Clothed
in Light

Clothed
in Light

by
Paul Jaffe

ELVIS PRESLEY ONLINE
GRASS VALLEY, CA

Elvis Presley Online
353 Pleasant Street
Grass Valley, California, 95945
(800) 378-6817
fax (800) 378-6821

First published in the United States—April 2000.

ISBN : 0-9672131-0-X (hc)
0-9672131-1-8 (pb)

Library of Congress Cataloging Number: 99-095427 (hc)
99-096606 (pb)

Design and production: Terragraphics, Berkeley, CA

For my mother, Rose,
and my father, Guss

"Man is a promise, he is not yet."

— the Talmud

Table of Contents

Clothed
in Light

Clothed in Light

My dying shocked me, although I don't know why. I mean it shouldn't of, I'd been killing myself for years. But I never wanted to admit it to myself. I always had lots of excuses. I guess most of us do. The morning I died I passed out about ten or eleven. The sun was high up in the sky. I was in my bathroom, indisposed as it were, when my insides buckled like a tin can. A light passed through my head and I was gone. There wasn't much pain. It was more like the life inside me drained out.

Then I came to. I didn't even know where I was at first. I saw my book on the floor, *The Scientific Search for the Face of Jesus,* and remembered I'd come in the bathroom to read cause I couldn't sleep. It was a good minute before I saw my body lumped face down on the floor in front of the toilet. I wasn't scared at all, that was the weird part. I just stood there wide awake about ten feet across the room. It took me a minute to realize I wasn't in my body anymore. It's strange seeing your body like this, like looking into a mirror and seeing somebody else. Although it seemed like I was attached to it, like I had the remote controls, but when I pushed the buttons, nothing happened. My mind was crystal clear, that was the weirdest part.

I tried to get back in my body but I couldn't. That's when I thought maybe I'd died. Then I thought, No way, if I died, I wouldn't be thinking about it. That was a good one. I wanted to use the little candle of my logical mind to light up a mystery so much bigger than my reason. But there I was, Sherlock Holmes, figuring away. Shows you how much I was used to running the whole show.

Then some lights appeared around the edges of my vision. They were bright little stars moving as if at the end of a magic wand, little spindles of light making slow arching turns and circling patterns. They were so beautiful, but more than that, these lights were utterly captivating. It was as if they were peace, or the emissaries of peace. The rays from the lights felt ancient, like they held the secret to existence. Their beams went through me. Course what I didn't realize was I'd entered a new body, one that could feel the penetrations of light.

It was like having everything you ever wished for. I thought, this is the peace that surpasses understanding. I'd spent most of my life trying to do this or be that; so seeing these lights, I knew I didn't have to do or be anything. It was hilarious. Reminded me of a dog who spends all his time sniffing around burying bones when his master plans on giving him an endless supply.

The bottles on the counter, the combs and tubes and brushes, the tiles of the shower, everything shone with a rosy light. The whole bathroom was a garden of light, like a masterpiece painting. All the stuff of the world was made of the same rosy light, just cut up in different-sized packages. The soaps and colognes, the towels and toothbrushes, even the lights and mirrors had personality. That's the effect the rosy light shining from everything had — it gave things a life. The colognes were sleek, kinda lanky and sexy, which cracked me up; the soaps seemed hardworking like they knew the value of a dollar. I was fascinated for the longest time by a tube of Colgate toothpaste on a folded towel. Everything about the little contours of the tube and folds of the towel told a story. I thought, I've seen this way before. It was when I was a little boy.

All the tension and uptightness I normally felt was gone. Obliterated. There was nothing to fear or resist, because everything was made of the same rosy light. Fear's always based on two. This overpowering that. When things are one, all fear disappears. A verse from the Sermon on the Mount came to me: "If thine eye be single, thy whole body shall be filled with Light." I closed my eyes and felt the light inside me. It was like I'd swallowed a star. It was love. All I'd ever wanted was love, and there it was streaming out of every single thing all along.

Soon Ginger, my girlfriend, knocked at the bathroom door and called for me. I wanted to holler that I was dying and everything was OK, but nothing came out. The bathroom door was far away like I was seeing it through the wrong end of a pair of binoculars. This was a painful moment. I was passing away. Ginger opened the door and saw me. I could read her mind. She knew right away I was dead but didn't want to believe it. She screamed and called downstairs. One of my men, Al Strada, ran in and I read his mind too. He thought I'd finally OD'd, which wasn't far off.

Everybody rushed in in a panic. I saw myself through my friends' eyes. My body was blue and a white foam covered my mouth. I was all blown-up. Bloated. I didn't wanna be in that body anymore. Joe Esposito came in and I felt better. He always knew what to do. Of course they tried to revive me. I felt like telling them not to worry. I wasn't scared and that was the strangest part because I'd always been afraid to die.

The paramedics arrived. Everybody was rushing around yelling, "Don't die, Elvis! Don't die." Everybody was scared. Fear's contagious, we catch it from each other easier than a cold. I had this panicky feeling like I'd done something wrong (dying!). I worried over everybody and how they were gonna manage without me. But then instead of spinning in tight little circles I went into a place of calm. Nothing could freak me out.

They put me on the stretcher to take me downstairs. I looked around my room and thought, this is the last time I'll see my bedroom. I felt nostalgic like I'd been dead for a hundred years. All my stuff — the furniture, my pictures, the bed — each thing had a life of its own. I cracked up. My gigantos bed looked bigger than some small countries. It had sad vibes too; it's where I'd gone to escape from the world. My TVs were funny and sad. I had three of 'em. They looked like the three stooges, Larry, Moe, and Curly. They'd been my windows to the world. I'd blocked out my real windows with tinfoil to keep the light out so I could sleep during the day. The few guns lying around the room gave me a shiver. They were full of power and fear and you couldn't help but look at them.

I saw my daughter, Lisa Marie, standing in the doorway. She'd heard the commotion and run to my room. She was bewildered and frightened. I broke down. It tore me up so much that I couldn't go to her. I didn't want to leave her. She was nine years old and needed me. More than anything, I didn't wanna leave my Yisa.

Lisa Marie was taken away downstairs. Talk about helpless, this was it: my heart was being ripped out of me and there was nothing I could do. Our souls spoke and she accepted what was happening better than me.

They wheeled me out of my room and down the stairs. I stood aside, outside my body, looking at the reflections people made in the mirrors. At first I didn't get why it was so fascinating. Then it hit me: all we are in life is images. The "alive" people huddled around my stretcher were nothing but images themselves. A life was an image cast into physical substance by the person's soul. Their souls had a much bigger life elsewhere. I could see it now, but none of them could.

There was nothing to do but surrender. It's quite a moment when you get that you're dead. I was going out, just like there'd been another moment, forty-two years before, when I'd come in in a little cabin in East Tupelo, Mississippi. So much had happened, enough for ten lifetimes, and here was the moment, the line of demarcation, for my life. I was leaving home for the last time, as we all do.

e   *e*   *e*

I looked around Graceland and thought about the good times — the Christmases, the nights around the piano, our dinners with everybody sparkling under the chandelier. The foyer been our karate dojo. I'd lived how I wanted — for better or worse. Nobody can ask for more than that. I loved Graceland. It was my refuge and palace; I coulda had a grander house, but not one sweeter. My heart was full, although I couldn't of told you if it was happiness or sorrow. I thought, I'm walking in beauty and truth.

I got rolled out the front door of Graceland and out into the heat. If you've never been to Memphis in summer, the heat's hard to imagine. Lemme put it this way: the sky feels like a huge, hot washrag laid all over you. It was steamy and still, the kind of weather that always made me wanna eat ice cream. As they carried me down the steps I thought about my boyhood in Tupelo. I was going out very close to where I'd come in.

I tried to reach people close to me, like Priscilla, who hadn't found out yet I'd passed over. It wasn't with words. It was feelings communicated through thought. It's how souls speak. There was nothing to hide anymore. I didn't feel shame, all I felt was love. I apologized to Priscilla for my lies and excuses, and for how things had gone. Our souls are cleansed by the truth. I felt no blame or guilt and my heart let go of its burden.

I stood aside as the paramedics put me in the ambulance. I knew the grounds of Graceland like the back of my hand, so what I didn't expect — what surprised me — was how everything looked. Things were so vivid, like a technicolor dream times ten. The veins in every leaf and blade sparkled and all the plants and trees shone in the light of creation. Everything living, from the tiniest blade of grass to the tall trees, pulsed with its own little breath. I thought the pulsing must be the wind, so I checked the tops of the trees. No movement. The tiny throbbing was the insides of things. I was seeing Spirit pump through matter, the divine energy that feeds and moves the world.

A hidden switch had been thrown and I'd entered a wonderland; that's how much brighter everything was. The bark on trees looked like miniature Grand Canyons. It had amazing depth and beauty like a Southwest landscape. I thought, how could I ever been bored?!

Then I heard a humming sound like a low-pitched roar and wondered if it was insects. I listened carefully, the humming wasn't bugs. It was the sound of the little breath inside of things, the low but steady roar of creation without beginning or end. It was ancient. I listened for the sound of "Om" I'd read about in metaphysical books but I didn't hear it. The humming was the sound of the "now" being born, the "always has been" giving birth to the "always will be."

My sense of time was shook up too. It only took a few seconds for the paramedics to load me into the ambulance, but it was time enough to see all this.

Forget about miracles, folks, how things come to be at all is miraculous. Creation didn't stop after seven days

— it's still going on! The world is born anew every second through divine light. The human eye can't see it, but if you could, it would look like a strobe flashing on and off as the world appears and disappears in flashes of light. Everything around you that seems so solid is really fluid as light — the chair you're sitting in, the shoes you're wearing, the tree out your kitchen window — all of it, everything, shares the same miracle of creation through light.

I was seeing the inside of things, the light inside of light, and it was beautiful and holy beyond description. I knew only one Sovereign could have created this beauty. God. When your soul reaches this point you know you've arrived at the truth and there's no room for doubts — God's taken them all away. Another scripture came to me. "His face shone like the sun, and His clothes became white as light." I was going to meet Him.

I felt God's presence before I saw Him. At once He appeared from where I do not know, putting His hand upon my shoulder. He spoke to me without words. All things great and small served but one purpose: love. Love was the alpha and the omega, and all things between.

God drew the sky down as you would a veil, covering us under a cloth of pearl. I'd seen Him a hundred times in my dreams, that silken hair, those bottomless eyes. Yet

I'd forgotten until this moment. God glowed from every pore and in His gaze was all knowledge. If I'd stacked all the great art of the world end to end it wouldn't of measured His beauty. I had never been without Him. I looked into God's eyes and knew it was Him whom I had longed for. All my life I'd wanted more of everything — more success, more money, more women — but it was Him whom I'd wanted. Every thought for something more had been a grasp for God.

God smiled at me. He knew my thoughts. The veil above us billowed in every direction. He spoke to me. "Once sought I am found. What eludes the night returns to the light of day. Fear not your wounds, heal and harvest them." He paused for His words to fill me and then He said, "Your heart and toil are planted in the Soul of man, Elvis, and they shall never perish. Your covenant has been fulfilled."

"What covenant has been fulfilled, Lord?" I asked.

God's thoughts became mine. I had brought to earth a seed of fate from heaven, as all men do. Its flowering was my life. My suffering and joy were branches of a single tree. I had wanted the sun and the bright of day, but it was in the arbor of His shadows where grace was found.

God brought me to truth and my heart broke open.

e   *e*   *e*

I was in this orange and white monster of an ambulance — man, that baby was huge. Joe, Charlie, and Dr. Nik climbed in with me. Needless to say they weren't in the greatest mood. Here I am expired on the stretcher but everybody's trying to bring me back — no matter that I'm deader than a doornail. But I got it. Saying goodbye was too heart-wrenching for the guys. I felt your love for me and it meant more than you can ever know.

I'd died yet there was no way I was dead. I was still alive. Death was something you passed through; it was just another experience and not the end of things. This is so important for you all to get. You go through death but you don't die. Death is but a marker on the greater path of your soul's life. Take it into all your considerations, into everything you think about your life, cause if you get just this one truth — YOU DON'T DIE — it will change your life. It will.

The paramedics flipped on the siren and we tore down the hill and through the music gates. They were taking me to Baptist Hospital. Everything was slowed down for me, the people moving on the sidewalks were like still photographs, every one a soul as if an open book to be read. All a person was, their hopes and fears and secrets, was in their light. People were vessels of light, and the Spirit I saw pouring outta folks was awesome. All things were made of light but humans were the brightest candle of creation. And it didn't have to do with somebody being young or beautiful, everybody had the same intense glow.

Nobody saw their light or beauty, though. They were blind and could not see. It was fascinating how people were, or weren't, themselves. I stopped being judge and jury. Whatever I saw in others had been true for me too.

Our siren split the traffic like Moses did the Red Sea. All things shone in the light of Spirit — the trees, and flowers, even the street signs — the world was clothed in light. Then I realized why people couldn't see the light. The surface of everything was covered with a thin film or grittiness. It was worry and fear and it lay over peoples' faces and bodies, over the buildings and trees and flowers, like a fine soot covering the light. The clouds in the sky were untouched, but that was about it. It wasn't dirt in a natural sense, it was all of mankind's accumulated pessimism and fear, passed from generation to generation, from person to person, like a hypnotic trance. It lay over the world like a dirty rag. The light shone through the grit; it was too bright to be blotted out, but people couldn't see it. Everybody was walking through paradise convinced they were in a solid waste dump.

The ambulance cut through the heat like a beast as we got on 240 downtown. I'd given up on telling the guys not to worry about me. They couldn't hear me. I wondered what I looked like. I was in a body, it just wasn't physical anymore. Didn't need a mirror to find out. Instant I asked the question a sense came. I was about twenty-one and in great shape, looking like that summer we moved into Audubon Drive, about the time of the big Russwood Park benefit, would have been '56. I was wearing a sportcoat I loved then; it was from Lansky's, cream colored with soft stripes and a velvet collar, lots of pockets. I wore that thing out, and now it was back.

The biggest change was how I saw myself. Lemme put it this way: my new body didn't have a defensive bone in it. I had no need, or interest, in justifying myself anymore, which was a minor miracle for yours truly. I suppose you could say I was stubborn, but that's too nice a spin, cause the truth is I was egotistical. In most things it was either my way or the highway. I got so pumped-up on fame and fortune that I couldn't even apologize when I was wrong. Even when I wanted to. I thought I was beyond the rules.

Death shrunk me to size. And what a relief it was to stop grinding my axe against the world. Weird as it sounds, dying's like smelling salts for your mind, clears you right up. I finally understood things I'd read about for years in Eastern religion and metaphysics. Everything on earth has its home in heaven, all things are themselves *and* a symbol for something greater in the beyond. Life is one huge work of art created by God for the purpose of our learning.

A river of truth runs through us. We hardly feel it but it's there. It's Soul flowing on and on. Call it the river of Soul or truth, doesn't matter, cause what it is is you without fear. We all sense this river and even feel it once in awhile. I did looking into a baby's eyes, especially my own little one. But we don't trust our souls enough, so we pass off wisdom as a fluke. There's a place in you that knows everything — and you're here to learn to trust it.

e   *e*   *e*

We might as well clear up right now how I died. To be honest, it was the drugs that did me in. At the end I felt a million years old and had seen and done it all — ten times. I'd been on automatic pilot for years, life by remote control. I'd press one metabolic button and go up, then I'd change the channel and press another and come down. After awhile it didn't matter what the channel was, they all had the same blank static. And to make it even weirder, I studied these medications like I was a pharmacist. I had the PDR by my bed, next to the clock, so I could tell you in a wink what all these drugs did. Still, I couldn't stop, although I could lay off and get straight for weeks at a time. I was in and out with it, and then ended up just being out. The last two years were the worst.

Wasn't anybody's fault. I don't wanna sound conceited, but it's almost impossible to describe what it was like being Elvis. I needed to relax and catch my breath — that, and I couldn't stand my family breaking up. That's where the drugs came in. I used to delude myself that I didn't have a drug problem because it was all coming from doctors. It was just an excuse. Prescription drugs, street drugs — same thing if you use 'em like I did.

It's not like it was a deep dark secret I was falling apart, it showed. My friends tried to help. Linda Thompson was a real trooper, and so was my cousin Billy. We were close. I was scared to death but I couldn't talk about it. I needed to be strong for everybody. If I wasn't Elvis where would we all be? That's what I thought about. I was suppose to be on top of the world and have it all together. I needed to talk and cry, that's all. Talk and cry.

I just didn't care enough. I was tired of being Elvis Presley. I'd think about stopping the prescriptions all the time, get in shape and feel really good, then I'd get bombed again cause something bad would happen. I pretended like I cared, but deep down I didn't.

Nothing much mattered so I took weird chances. If I died or overdosed, so what. I'm embarrassed to admit it, but that's how I felt. I didn't wanna die or commit suicide. It's more complicated than that. I walked away from the rudder of my life and just watched what happened.

Nothing's more boring than drugs, even though some people think they're glamorous. You're a robot programming yourself for one thing: not to feel what you feel, and that's completely ass-backwards, folks. It's only by feeling what you feel that you are who you are. I became something I wasn't. Once that happens, who cares?

What happened was a bad combination of drugs, the ones I usually took combined with the codeine my dentist gave me the night before. I'd had allergic reactions to codeine before but for some reason I forgot. When you don't care, bad things happen. You forget what you need to remember. That's what happened to me 16 August 1977. But if it hadn't happened that day it would've some other.

This is where I think about Momma. I could always talk with her, no matter what I was feeling. She felt the same with me. Being with Momma was the one place I felt understood. When she died I lost that. That part of me died too. Didn't have to be that way, but that's how it was.

Take the path of heart and courage every time, and you'll never look back.

e   *e*   *e*

Everybody in the ambulance was solemn thinking about what I'd meant to them. I knew what the paramedics were thinking. We swung off the Union exit, Baptist Hospital was just up ahead. They had their own memories of me, like being with a sweetheart when "Hound Dog" came on the radio, or how "Heartbreak Hotel" summed up something they'd gone through, stuff like that. I was a part of these guys, part of the great Soul that flowed on the earth. It was like a prayer and it made me humble.

When we die it's not just our memory that gathers inside those who've loved us. Our very self is displayed, constellated like a star, within the souls of our loved ones. We're connected, all of us to each other, through paths of love that words can never describe. There's more love in the world than you can ever imagine.

Little memories drifted through me soft as snow as we stopped in front of the emergency room doors. I thought, Man, I've been spending too much time here. Except for the birth of Lisa Marie, Baptist Hospital was a pretty sad place for me, like drawing the Go-to-Jail card in Monopoly. Over the years I'd come here to rest, worn out from being Elvis. Good doctors would come to my bedside, talk to me about the results of tests, give me information I already knew. I'd look out the window and feel the world passing me by. Wasn't taking care of myself, needed to cut down on this or that medication. Most of the doctors were polite, very bright men who were a little bit in awe of me. They didn't need to be. If they'd known how I felt, what a scared guy with health problems I was, they wouldn't of been star-struck no more.

Once we hit the emergency room entrance, the action began. A VIP had arrived. They went into their codes. Everybody got to work. When they're trying to save your life it ain't pretty. There were humorous moments. A young nurse turned to one of the doctors and asked why in the world they were working so hard on a corpse. The doctor said, "Because he's Elvis Presley." Everybody nodded and kept working away. When they finally gave up, next stop for me was Autopsy. I couldn't see any point in hanging around for that, and as soon as I decided to split, I was with those amazing, angelic lights again.

They came together into one big shining light, an enormous star that came to rest just above my brow, bathing me. There wasn't any heat. The light was cool and soft and serene. It began to dissolve me into itself. I was the light, too. Time ceased.

Jessie

It'd be easy for you to make too much of me, see me as a big star, larger than life, and cause of that different from you. But I'm not. I stumbled plenty in my life and hurt the way we all do. Matter of a fact, one reason I'm telling my story is cause people make too much of stars. Putting somebody on a pedestal only makes you smaller, and then you miss altogether the grandeur inside yourself. Besides, I had about as many problems as a man can have, so there's no reason for me to be on anybody's pedestal.

Where do I start? There's so much to say I considered not speaking at all. Does my voice add or subtract from the confusion of the world? Everything in time has its moment, though, and this is the time for my heart to speak. My hope is pretty simple: to lighten somebody's burden and lift their eyes to the horizon where eternity shines. I always wandered around and through things, backwards, forwards, skipping this, adding that, letting things make their own crazy sense. Mine was the way of water, I got to know something by flowing with it, letting it become a part of me.

e   *e*   *e*

As a kid, I'd lie in bed at night and listen to the silence. It was loud like a roar and I'd travel out on it, try to feel its end, but I could never find where it stopped. I thought the silence was forever, the everlasting. I'd listen for sounds — the backfire of a car or a rogue rooster — and ride them until they disappeared back into the silence. It was like a train that never ran out of tracks. In my mind I'd see an ancient ocean pounding away on a faraway planet.

Everything was alive when I was little. One of my favorite things was watching clouds move across the sky — the springtime was best cause then the clouds were towers growing all the way to heaven — I saw kings and queens and knights of the Round Table, armies stretching across the sky. There'd be battles, and feasts, and celebrations. I'd whisper to Jessie, my twin brother who died at our birth, and he'd tell me the stories that went along with the clouds.

For Momma and me, Jessie's dying only made him live forever. I even saw Jessie when I was little. I was playing in the woods and he appeared beside me. That happened a couple of times. He looked just like me but in different clothes. By the way, Jessie's grave was right there, in East Tupelo, he wasn't buried out at Priceville Cemetery. He was across the way down by the creek, under a giant weeping willow full of songbirds. I took a friend there sometimes, James Ausborn; ask him about it, he'll tell you.

I'd go to Jessie's grave and talk out my troubles. It always made me feel better the same as prayer. There'd be so many birds in the branches of that willow. It sounded like an aviary. It was Jessie and me at the top of the world. I'd whisper to him and he'd answer me in my heart.

Aunt Rhetha

It was a foggy day and cold and I was in the bathtub when Aunt Lillian came over to tell Momma about Aunt Rhetha. I was six years old.

I heard Momma open the front door. She saw her face and said, "Oh, my God." Aunt Lillian looked dark as death.

I heard Momma shout, "Something's happened. Oh Lord in heaven help us, look at you!" Her voice was bleating, like a lamb's.

Aunt Rhetha's coal oil stove had blown up and burnt her. I heard Daddy holler, "Oh my God, no! No!"

They'd taken Aunt Rhetha to Tupelo Hospital.

I closed my eyes in the tub. I was blue inside, and cold. The little boats on the water looked far away like they were out on the ocean. I heard them say Aunt Rhetha was still alive. I felt like I'd disappeared but still I could see. There was a bare oak high up in the little window of the bathroom, naked and slick in the fog. I smelled it through the wall. It smelled cold and musty. My little-boy mind tried to reckon death. All things die, I thought, everybody has to die. The light bulb flickered and popped, and went out. I jumped out of the tub and dried off, shivering to the bone. It felt like the devil was watching me put my clothes on.

I stepped into the light of the kitchen. "Is Rhetha gonna live?" Momma asked. Amongst all her sisters she felt closest to Rhetha. They were about the same age and grew up together. I stood on a chair next to her and looked into her face. She came to a cry but couldn't. Her soul knew Rhetha was gonna die.

Everything was so still; it was like time had stopped, the pots and pans, the jars on the shelves, seemed unnatural and lopsided. Aunt Lillian stood under the light and shadows fell over her. She washed her tongue around the inside of her mouth and didn't say anything. She was the oldest and mother to everybody.

"How bad's her burn?" Daddy said. His voice was shaking. "A real bad burn, it's better for God to take them." Inside, his chest felt like a hot poker from stuffing his feelings down. He rocked back and forth in his stocking feet and long underwear and looked up at the ceiling, not knowing what to say. I went over and touched his hand and he hugged me.

A train crossed the levee and shook the house. I wanted something to happen, somebody cry, scream, anything! but everybody was too froze up.

The sunset came through the windows of the kitchen and I felt Aunt Rhetha. I thought, she can see us. And she did, I was right. I thought about my cousin Harold, Rhetha's son, and wondered where he'd go. Harold was twelve.

Momma stared at the floor and rubbed her hands together like she was washing at the sink. Her face was stiff as a piece of plaster. It was shock, all the blood had run out of her. "I'll get my coat," she said. I was scared and wanted to scream. Nobody looked at me. They just talked amongst themselves.

Aunt Lillian came to Momma and put her arm around her. Momma closed her eyes like she wanted to sleep, but there was no forgetting this.

"I'll stay here with Elvis," Daddy said. His voice came from far away. "Where's Harold, was he at home?" he asked.

Aunt Lillian said, "He's over with Clettes and Vester, they'll stay with the kids." Aunt Lillian looked so big inside her coat, like the angel of death.

I was scared to let Momma go. I grabbed her around the waist and buried my face in her skirt. I thought she'd die too and I held her tight.

Aunt Lillian came over and pulled me away. I didn't want to cry in front of her and get a scolding. Momma knelt down to my face. "Everything's gonna be OK, honey. Stay here with your daddy, or go over to your

Aunt Clettes and Uncle Vester's."

"We'll stay here for now," Daddy said, "we'll wait for what you say. Go on to Rhetha, Elvis and me'll be fine. If Vester goes to the hospital tell him to stop on his way back. We'll pray for Rhetha. This is an awful day." Daddy was twenty-five years old.

He didn't want the lights. He lit a couple of lamps and turned them down low. I was scared our coal-burner would blow too. I wanted more lights but didn't say anything. Daddy sat by himself. If he was upset, he never wanted anybody.

I waited for Momma to come back and thought about Aunt Rhetha. She was my favorite aunt. She and Momma were the cut-ups in the family, the jokesters. She was gonna die, I could feel it. Saturday mornings Aunt Rhetha'd make Harold and me pans of cinnamon rolls with raisins. I gotta remember the smell of those rolls baking in the oven and never forget, I thought. Car lights came down Kelly Street and jumped shadows up the walls. Rhetha'd tell stories at our picnics on the ground after church. She'd tell about Momma and her as girls and how they'd picked flowers and strung 'em through their hair and danced like princesses through the forest. The kids had been dirt-poor, working from dawn to dusk just to survive. Her eyes would shine and Rhetha'd do a little dance; then she'd hunker up her shoulders and play

Aunt Lillian scolding Momma and her. Aunt Lillian would laugh too. Aunt Rhetha's in heaven now, so there's no reason to cry, I thought.

I asked Daddy, "Is Aunt Rhetha dead?" I wanted him to talk to me but he didn't say anything. The crickets were so loud outside I wanted to cover my ears.

Aunt Rhetha's burns were too much. She died that night. Momma rocked back and forth on the sofa, quiet as a church mouse, wringing her hands like she was washing. It'd been too many deaths, too many losses for her. Her father and mother, Grandma Anna, and now Rhetha. I asked after what she wanted, a drink of water or a pillow for her legs, but she didn't want anything. It went on like this for a week. It scared me to death, I thought she'd lost the ability to speak. I didn't know what to do.

Then she went to a meeting, a Holiness revival, at Union Grove. She took the bus over to Parkertown, by herself, to see a famous preacher who was passing through. I'll tell you this, it was an altogether different woman who came back from that meeting.

The revival lasted most of the night, so I didn't see her till the next morning. I woke up and heard her beating pancakes. Her back was turned but I could tell she was feeling better without even seeing her face.

"You sit down, Elvis," she said, "these flapjacks will be ready in a minute. I chopped up some pecans and you can have 'em with cinnamon and syrup."

I thought, her voice is back, maybe now she knows Aunt Rhetha's in heaven.

"You're feeling better, Momma, I can tell," I said. "Your voice ain't quiet this morning. Can I have 'em with cinnamon and sugar with syrup on top?"

"However you want, honey. Lord, isn't it a beautiful morning. Look at this sun shine in the kitchen after all the fog we've had. Spring's right around the corner." The light was the same as what I saw when I died — that light inside of light — it pooled up on the kitchen table and I washed my hands in it.

"The trees got flowers on 'em, Momma. There's a pink one in the yard got a mess of flowers. I'm gonna go frogging today. All the tadpoles done become frogs, there's a million of 'em at the pond. They was loud last night. Me and Daddy listened to 'em."

"That's a dogwood, Elvis. You be careful down at the pond. You don't go swimming now, you don't know how."

"Why do they call 'em dogwoods? Is there some dog they named after?"

"I don't rightly know," she laughed, "ask somebody else. Here's your pancakes, lemme get you some silverware and a napkin. The bacon'll be ready in a minute. I'll make it crispy old toast like you like it."

I put gobs of fresh butter and maple syrup on my stack of pancakes. One thing about Tupelo, the food was out of this world. My mother sat down with her plate and ate.

"I went to Union Grove last night." The sun was beautiful on her face. She didn't have a wrinkle. "It was a preacher from Alabama, a Pastor Henry. He was a young man, a football player at some college awhile back. The Lord's touched him, Elvis, Pastor Henry's got the gift of prophecy."

"Uh huh."

"It was like the old days. Folks got up and testified, there was a bunch of people traveling with Pastor Henry. Folks were jerking and barking in tongues, going to Jesus. Pastor Henry knew about Rhetha. I think it was the Swayzes that told him. He said Jesus knew the burden of my heart, and I should give it to Him and be healed. I was to know the truth of death: that's what Jesus wanted for me. I felt the Holy Spirit come into me, Elvis. He was a blue mist and bright as a pearl. Pastor Henry laid hands on me. He called on Jesus to show me the truth of death. I saw, Elvis. I saw what death is. It's a stairway to heaven."

"Uh huh." I said. I listened close.

"All those tears I been holding back for Rhetha, they all came out. The Swayzes came to me, and the Randles. It was like a river of tears rushing through me. I felt Rhetha in heaven. I could almost touch her. She's in glory, blazing in light beside the Lord. Oh Elvis, the colors I saw, honey, it was more beautiful than anything in this world!"

"Yes."

"Jessie was there, with Aunt Rhetha. He's an angel in heaven, Elvis, he's looking out for us. Your brother sees us down here."

"I been talking to him, Momma."

"Praise the Lord, darling. You're identical twins, Elvis, you're the same. He's in heaven and you're down here on earth. He's always with you. That's what he said."

"I know."

"Well, he's looking out for you, Elvis. And all the strength of two has gone into you, honey. That's what I heard Jessie say. All the strength of two.

"But that wasn't all. Pastor Henry, and what a good-looking man he was, tall and strong like a football player with such beautiful brown hair ... he said I'd been touched by God with Jessie and Rhetha dying, and you, Elvis, would know the riches of Spirit and worldly success. He said he saw you in front of crowds of people. You'll be a leader. That's what he said, and I knew it was true. I've known it. I've told you that."

"Yes," I said. "I know it too, Momma."

Memphis

I was thirteen when we moved from Tupelo to Memphis. It was the fall of 1948. We'd talked so much about moving to Memphis it was a relief to get it over with. We were broke and it was time to go. I got home from school one day, we were on North Green Street, and my Mom and Dad were sitting at the kitchen table in the middle of the afternoon, talking. I knew something was up, they never did that. Momma came over and put her arm around me. "Honey," she said, "your daddy lost his job. There's nothing left for us here. We're gonna move to Memphis, it'll be better for you there." She was trying to be brave but I felt her fear. I was just glad they hadn't left the decision up to me.

My Dad said the same thing, Memphis would give me a chance. He was talking about himself. Tupelo been hard for him, he always felt unappreciated there. I didn't care that much, Tupelo was all I knew. It was different for my parents, though. They felt like they'd failed, like Tupelo had broke them. But it wasn't Tupelo, it was poverty. Worn 'em down flatter than the Delta. We left the next day. The cord had to be cut quick or we never coulda done it.

The day we moved they argued and made up all day long. Momma was doing her master sergeant routine. It was, "Elvis, don't forget this, and have you done that? Don't forget to pack all your underwear, honey." She did the same to my Dad, only she was harder on him. "Don't over-pack the top of the car, Vernon. Did you feed the chickens, and how 'bout the dogs?" He got mad, flustered, but he never knew what to say. She was scared and being a mother hen gave her something to do. Momma always wanted change, said she wanted things to be different, then change would come and it be too much.

Family came to say good-bye and she burst into tears. My Dad was upset too except he kept it inside. He had a faraway look in his eyes, like in shock. I found him around the side of the house that afternoon. He was fixing some machinery he'd sold, oiling a winch and tightening up a pump. He was sitting on ground the chickens had pecked clean, piling up dirt in little mounds and looking off into space. I knelt down beside him but he didn't see me. He looked like a little boy. I didn't know what to say, he seemed so far away. Finally I asked, "How long we been here?"

He said, "I don't know. What do you mean, us or the whole family?"

"The family, how long we been in Tupelo anyway?" I said.

He shook his head a long time. "I don't know, nobody can remember." He was thinking about times as a boy, walking the woods in summer, the sunlight crisscrossing through the tall trees. He remembered his young body, the spring dogwood and azaleas, the earth looking like the first days of man. Those little mounds of dirt were his goodbye. He was thinking about the land, he wasn't thinking about people.

We packed the ol' humpbacked Plymouth to the gills. Top of the car looked like a furniture mart. It was exciting. Hundred miles straight up Highway 78 — Memphis. We drove through the night like into a dream.

e   *e*   *e*

Memphis was a shock. Instead of pastures there were streets, and the country was a vacant lot with a lonely tree or two. At first we stayed in rooming houses downtown on the northside, first on Washington then over on Poplar. The place on Poplar was a big ol' four story

Victorian that been cut up into rooms. Never lived so close to people.

We had one room. There was a bed and a love seat, a chair and a table, one skinny window that let in a thimbleful of light. The floorboards were all scuffed like a million people had passed through. We shared a bathroom with the whole floor, cooked on a hot plate. The only spigot was in the bathroom and you turned green when you looked at it. My parents would sit at the table underneath the window and read the want ads. My dad be in his Ben Davis workshirts with that silly monkey, and my mom in her flower dresses. They'd read a want ad out loud — the sheer possibility of it would hang in the air — then we'd laugh. It was better than crying. We kept the newspapers and stacked 'em up.

"Maybe I should go back to Armour and see if they're hiring." That was one my dad's favorite riffs. "Cook me some bacon. Barbecue hot dogs!" He'd say it with a little grin on his face. During the war he'd worked at Armour Meat, come back to Tupelo on weekends. He'd been a fry cook and hated it.

They'd go through their little ritual though. Momma would say, "You don't know, you gotta keep checking back, that's how you land a job." He'd nod but both of them knew he wasn't going back to Armour.

Those rooming houses were bleak, man, I'd get to feeling weird like the walls were bulging in on me. The furniture'd get real big and crazy like something outta a horror movie. It felt like a hundred-pound weight was squishing my head and I'd get a headache and need air. For a break I'd take walks up and down Poplar, look out on the streets and try to remember the pastures and forests of Tupelo. It was wintertime and I was lonely. That first winter was the hardest. Felt chilled to the bone half the time and lonely the rest. I liked walking. It calmed me down and cleared my head. Mostly walked by myself. Momma like to stay put and my daddy wasn't there but half the time. I didn't know anybody in Memphis. I felt less lonely walking around.

I see myself thirteen years old, walking around Memphis. I'm shy and a little scared, with big eyes that wanna swallow the world.

e　　　　　*e*　　　　　*e*

The move to Memphis jacked my energy big-time. My body started jumping, I mean literally; my leg picked up a wiggle even when I was sitting still. It wasn't teenage hormones either. I didn't know what to make of it, but now I see what happened. Cities, any place you have a mess of people, are vortexes of energy — force fields —

if you're sensitive, and I was, moving into one of these vortexes boots your energy right up. Probably sounds like science fiction, but it's spiritual fact.

I felt like I'd been dropped on Mars, that's how different everything in Memphis was. We were living only a couple of blocks from Main Street, and lemme tell you, it was some street then. There were millions of shops and people everywhere — theaters, hotels, restaurants — pool halls and pawn shops lined the street like stepping stones. This was before shopping malls sucked everybody out to the suburbs. A walk up Main Street in Tupelo made me ready for a nap, but Memphis was a whole different venue. There was enough energy on the streets to raise the dead.

There might of been a million shops with things to buy, but we didn't have any money. Couldn't buy a thing. It made me humble, which was good; later on my spending turned into an ego trip. I couldn't buy enough. Weird, you go without and it makes you appreciate, then you get whatever you want and you're still not satisfied.

At least I gave money away. Although that got crazy too. I'd get depressed and try to spend my way out of it. I bought thirty cars in a week once. Gave 'em all away. I'm serious. Generosity's one thing, but I was just plain nuts. It was the drugs. I'd get a fool idea and then who was gonna stop me. It was weird, being Elvis, you could do pretty much whatever you wanted.

My Mom and Dad found work, my momma over at Fashion Curtain as a seamstress and Daddy got on at Precision Tool. He'd worked there during the war. We had to celebrate. We went to a Saturday matinee and then dinner at Britling's Cafeteria. It was a sunny day in January, 1949. We walked from the rooming house on Poplar up Main Street to the Malco Theater. We got dressed up, my daddy and me in white shirts and slacks — they might of been hand-me-downs but they were cleaned and pressed — and Momma in a navy blue dress she'd sewn herself with a white, satin-flowered hat. She found the hat in a thrift store for a quarter; it was an expensive hat, and she loved it. I was so proud of us, we hardly ever did things as a family.

The Malco was one of the oldtime theaters with chandeliers and velvet handrails and those curlicue flowers all over the walls. The line out front to get tickets was a half-a-block long. My mom and dad held hands, things were always better between them when they had jobs. We got our tickets and went inside. What a palace. The lights and colors, the carpet was so thick my feet thought the floor was clouds. It was "The Treasure of the Sierra Madre" with Humphrey Bogart. We found seats middle front and waited for the movie to begin. I'd never seen anything like the Malco, you could've fit four or five of Tupelo's little theaters in it.

In the movie Bogart plays a roughneck kind of character who strikes it rich, but the gold drives him crazy. It was neat watching Bogie turn into a paranoid flip-case. He ends up losing his gold when the dust falls on the ground. A windstorm blows it away. "Dust to dust," Momma said, "the money drove Bogie crazy."

"Vernon, let's go over and see the Peabody Hotel." We were out front of the Malco deciding what to do after the movie. "They say it's the South's finest hotel. It'd be good for Elvis to see it. We can see how the other half lives."

"Why not?" Daddy said, "It don't cost anything to walk through the place. We're presentable. It's close by, I think, a couple of blocks away." He'd worked in Memphis for years and never gone into the Peabody.

"I've been there," I said. "Just from the outside walking by. Follow me, I know where it is."

I took them over to the Peabody, an old building of granite and marble that took up a whole block just north of Beale Street. The Peabody was society, the old South; William Faulkner, the great author, used to stay there when he was in Memphis. Cotton money is what made Memphis, it was the cotton capital of the world in the forties. Then, businessmen were in and out of the Peabody like a revolving door.

There were flags and flowers and a bustle of people at the entrance to the hotel. The black doormen smiled and bowed, opening the glass doors with their long, white gloves. I wasn't ready for how grand the hotel was. There were pillars of beige marble the size of tree trunks and carved-wood beams running the length of the ceiling; a bunch of crystal chandeliers hung from a stain-glass dome, and in the middle of the room was a fountain, with ducks. That impressed me, I gotta say, I couldn't figure how they kept the ducks from messing the place.

Daddy said, "The other half looks like they're living pretty good, Gladys." My dad had a dry sense of humor.

The three of us craned our necks looking up at the mezzanine portico that framed the lobby. The hotel smelled of leather and cigar smoke, and ladies' perfume, the couches and chairs were calfskin leather the color of tobacco leaf. I ran my hand over a chair and it was so smooth and cool under my fingers.

"Isn't it the most gorgeous thing you've ever seen?" Momma said. "They probably have your debutante balls here, all the society things. I betcha if a movie star came to Memphis, Elvis, this'd be the place they'd stay." Momma loved Hollywood and glamour. We always had movie magazines around the house growing up, every-time we moved in Tupelo we lugged a crate of 'em along with us.

Everbody in the hotel was dressed up, the men in coats and ties and hats and the women in silk dresses with alligator purses. It was like a scene from a movie, we musta looked like three bumpkins who'd just fell off the sweet potato truck. We walked through the lobby, and down a marble corridor of expensive jewelry and hi-fashion stores. Momma and me stopped and window-shopped, pointing at all the beautiful things. Daddy drifted off by himself and leaned up against a marble pillar.

He stood there with his arms crossed, his blue eyes blank as a cat's. All the rich people and expensive things made him feel bad. But my dad never showed his feelings. He was a handsome man, six-foot-two with wavy blond hair, but he didn't have any faith in himself. When he'd been my age, his daddy, Grandpa Dee, beat him and sent him away. He called my dad a good-for-nothing, lazy lout. After that my dad quit trying.

Momma waved my daddy over to take a look at a diamond ring in the jewelry store window. It had a pink-blue fire, about a carat and a half, that made it stand out. My dad looked at the ring and sucked his cheeks. "Vernon," Momma said, "we're going in the store next door and look at the new clothes. Why don't you come on in with us?"

"Why?" he said. "We can't buy anything."

"I just wanna see the fashions they're showing this year. You don't have to buy anything to go in the store, let's just go in and enjoy ourselves and have a look." She was always trying to get my dad to join us. I couldn't figure it out. He loved her more than anything.

"You go in with Elvis," he said. "I'm gonna wander over yonder and see what else is in the hotel. I'll meet you all back here in a half-hour or so."

Momma and me shopped for awhile, then we met up with my Dad and decided to go to supper. We walked through the lobby and saw the ducks marching away from the fountain and following to a jazz band playing "When the Saints Go Marching In." We stopped and watched 'em waddle out single file; they reminded me of little bales of cotton marching out of Memphis. It was the funniest thing you'd ever seen.

As we left the hotel an advertisement on a sandwich board caught Momma's eye. "Look here, Vernon," she said, "there's gonna be a big band dance contest on top of the hotel, in the Skyway Room." She put a hand on the sandwich board and kicked one leg in the air behind her, balancing on her other leg, graceful as a seal. She smiled her best beauty queen smile for me and my Dad.

My Dad said, "I oughta get a camera, Gladys. That's a picture if I ever saw one."

She put her leg down and said, "Think we should go, Vernon. Says right here the best couple wins a hundred dollar prize." When she got excited my momma was beautiful. "You and me could practice at home on the Victrola. We might win, who knows?" She put her hands on her thighs and hiked up her skirt, and kicked-up her heels again, smiling like Betty Grable at the USO.

The picture of her leaning on that sandwich board stuck with me; thirty years later, falling asleep at Graceland, I still saw her in front of the Peabody. It was all the movie magazines around our house, Fred Astaire and Ginger Rogers, Clark Gable and Bette Davis, dancing and riding horses, lounging around in slinky dresses and smoking jackets, looking into each other's eyes. Hollywood was my momma's dream, that's why she collected the magazines — it made that life seem close for her. She had talent too. My mother could sing and dance. She wanted to be a Hollywood star.

Over dinner at Britling's we talked about Humphrey Bogart and what he could of done if the money hadn't driven him crazy. The cafeteria had my favorites: chicken-fried steak, crowder peas, and banana pudding. What a wonderful day it'd been.

The Courts

The end of that first summer in Memphis, would've been '49, we caught a good break; we got to move into the Courts, the public housing works on Lauderdale and Winchester on the north side of downtown. It felt like we had a home again. The Courts were nothing fancy, red brick and three stories, kinda like a military base. There were lawns and shade trees and big magnolias, and the breezes would come up off the river. The Mississippi was only three blocks away. There was a ton of kids and we played for hours out on the mall, the big lawn that ran down the middle of the Courts. We were all struggling and poor, but these were good times nevertheless.

I made some great friends at the Courts, Bobby Ford, Harley Buy, and Dirk Dougher. We had our own little rat pack, the four musketeers. We'd go uptown and roam around for hours, shop, play pool, hang out in Court Square and people-watch; or we'd check out the girls at Malone Pool, the public swimming pool a few blocks from the Courts.

I'll tell you one thing, we weren't big spenders. We worked hard for every penny, doing odd jobs, mowing lawns in the summer with an ol' push mower and cutting weeds with a half-moon sickle. We shopped something till *it* dropped. We'd check out a half-dozen stores for the best price on a pair of Levi's or a shirt. Knew every cheap movie in town too. We'd get in the Suzores for a dime, popcorn was a nickel. It was like TV, we'd watch whatever was on — westerns with Gary Cooper or Alan Ladd, Tarzan or King Kong — it was great as long as you didn't mind sharing your popcorn with an occasional rat.

Those times hanging-out in Court Square were some of the funniest. Our teenage minds hatched some bizarre situations. Like the day Bobby Ford and me were going back and forth, ranking on each other. You all call it trash-talking today. Bobby was a good ol' boy, sturdy, but he had a geeky side too. Anyway, he says to me, "Elvis, you're about the ugliest dude in this park 'cept for that ol' dog sleeping over yonder under the bench. No, I take it back, I see now that hound has a nice profile."

I said, "Bobby, if I looked like you, last thing I'd want is to bring up looks. I heard your mother calling for you yesterday while she was staring at a trash can."

"Shut up you guys." Dirk Dougher jabbed me in the ribs. "Look over there at those two. Man, they beauty queens or what?" Our eyes went to two young ladies, in skirts and sweaters, strolling at the angel fountain. "What grade you think they're in? You seen 'em around before? They're probably seniors." Dirk was a hopeless romantic, I mean far gone. "I think I'm in love," he says.

Bobby says, "I'll take you to the movies tonight if you go over and ask one of 'em for a date, Elvis." He had a grin that reminded you of an oversized cob of corn. Bobby loved egging people on. Boy could hardly contain himself. "And if you get to first base, I'll carry your books to school, for a week." He was panting by this time.

"Shut up, Bobby," I said. "You can't carry my books anywhere. People would think we're going together. That's the last problem I need."

I did feel like going over and talking to the girls, particularly the little brunette in the tight skirt. She had blue eyes and a cute nose, little older than me. I hadn't seen her around school and there was no way I would have missed her. "OK," I said, "but you guys gotta back me up whatever I say, hear me?" Their faces nodded up and down like noodles dangling from a fork. "Whatever I say now, it's gotta be gospel, OK?"

I took a deep breath and started walking toward the girls, wondering if they could see my adam's apple bobbing outta my throat. I got to the fountain and stood a few feet away from them. The sound of the water calmed me. I tried to think of something to say but couldn't. Finally I said the first thing that popped into my head. "How you all this afternoon? Looking things over, getting ready for Cotton Carnival? It's not long now, next month." I prayed they'd say something cause I had no idea what to say next.

They looked at each other and giggled. The little brunette was blushing. The other girl had brown hair and fine features, Scandinavian looking. She answered, "I guess so. I know we'll go. We haven't really thought about it, huh, Julie?"

Julie spoke, "No, but I always go." She was perfect, a little prim and a little sassy. "How about you?" she asked, looking right at me.

"Sure I'll be going," I said. "Spring practice oughta be over by then, so I'll have time."

"Spring practice? Are you on the football team?" They both said it at once. I don't know what it was with me, practical joking or just being scared, but as a kid I'd get in situations like this and make things up.

"Yes, I am. My name's Owen Smith and I play end for Humes High, my friends sitting over there are my team-mates." I pointed over to Bobby and Dirk. They waved back.

"I'm Julie Christian, and this is Diana Gustafson. We go to East." They looked it. Their clothes were expensive. East High was a rich kids' school out on Poplar, *east*

Poplar. "We're pom-pom girls. I don't think I remember seeing you with the Humes team though, Owen."

"Naw, I always keep my helmet on, you never know when somebody's gonna hit you. It's a rough game." I was getting in deeper, but that's how it goes with a lie. I was just hoping they wouldn't ask more questions.

"We'll have to look for you next year, Owen. What's your number? I felt Julie's eyes on me. She liked me. I thought, oh swell, here's this gorgeous girl interested in me and I'm ruining everything with a fool lie.

"It's — it's — it's changing next year." Whenever I was nervous I stuttered. I glanced back to see Dirk and Bobby walking toward us.

They stopped and waited for an introduction. I was tongue-tied. Finally Julie spoke, "Owen says you all on the Humes football team. I'm Julie and this is Diana, we're pom-pom girls at East." Diana said "Hi."

Well, you never saw such willing liars in your life. They started in with touchdowns they'd run, interceptions to win games, the whole disaster. I just wanted 'em to back me up, and now they'd turned into pathological liars.

They got done with their highlights and everybody looked at me for my mine. I was sick. Here, I liked Julie, and maybe she liked me, but it was hopeless, there was no way out except to tell the truth and beg for mercy. I started to, but I couldn't. I was too embarrassed. I looked at everybody and said, "Yeah, it's gonna be a great season. I can't wait."

Bobby says, "Tell 'em about your ninety yard run, Owen."

I couldn't take it anymore. Could only see things going downhill. I said, "Guys, we're suppose to be over at the Oddfellows by now, aren't we? What time is it? We gotta go." I grabbed Bobby and Dirk by the arm and started walking away.

Julie waved goodbye. It was sad. "Hope I see you at the Humes game, Owen," she called, "or maybe at Cotton Carnival."

The Oddfellows was just next door in the Columbia Mutual Tower. We went upstairs to play some pool. Played eight ball for awhile, but my heart wasn't in it. I asked Dirk and Bobby if they felt like taking a trip up the elevator to check out the view. The Columbia Mutual Tower was the tallest building in town and had a great view of the Mississippi. Up the elevator we went, clunkity-clunk, to the 25th floor. Stepped out and there was the Mississippi winding down the Delta in the spring sun. Like always, we looked around to see if anybody was coming. Then we opened the windows and leaned way out, wedging our thighs hard against the bottom of the windowsills so we wouldn't fall. The wind blew our hair straight up like a rollercoaster ride. Dirk and Bobby's grins were priceless. We were three teenage maniacs waving our hands above our heads from the highest perch in Memphis. I thought about lying to Julie and screamed.

Billie Wardlaw moved to the Courts above us, on the third floor. She was shy and wouldn't come out at first. Sat up in her window and watched us play out on the mall. She reminded me of a young señorita up in her balcony, all that dark hair coming down around her face. Kinda like Tyrone Power's girlfriend in The Mark of Zorro. It was love at first sight for me.

I'd call up to her window, "Why don't you come down and play with us?"

"I can't," she'd say, "don't got the right clothes." She was just scared and wondering where she fit in. I knew cause I'd felt the same way when I got to Memphis. You come to the big city and wanna make a good impression.

If Billie was in her window, I made sure I was out there playing, looking outta the side of my eye to see if she was watching me. I kept trying to coax her down, but she stuck to the same excuse: "Don't got the right clothes."

One night as I was about to fall asleep, I figured out what to do. I had some money I was saving up for school clothes. I'd buy her a pair of jeans. Billie'd love 'em and it kill two birds with one stone — she'd have her clothes *and* know I was serious. Next day, right after school, I went up to Main Street and bought her some Levi's, new ones from Goldsmith's. I was so excited I ran all the way home with the package. I sprinted up the stairs and stood there in front of her door trying to calm down. My heart was thumping out of my chest. I knocked on the door. She opened it. I put the present behind my back so she couldn't see it.

"Elvis, how are you? You're all out of breath, how come you been running?" She smiled and leaned up against the doorjamb. Billie was different at home than school, more relaxed. She was wearing a faded green country dress that reminded me of Tupelo. Billie had a quiet disposition, she was tall and had a slender face and peaceful blue eyes, she didn't talk much unless she knew you. She was just a girl and hadn't realized yet how beautiful she was.

"I bought you something, a present." I was so nervous my voice croaked.

"You did?" She said it with a little tease in her voice. I settled a bit, she was happy I was at her door with a present. Her long black hair fell in waves over her shoulders.

She said, "You shouldn't be buying me no presents, Elvis. Why'd you go and do that?"

"Cause I wanted to, that's why," I said.

"Well, where is it, behind your back?" she said.

I switched the package behind my back and brought my free hand out, palm up. "Nope, not behind my back. See, no present." I loved teasing her, it was the fastest way to Billie's heart.

Billie grabbed my other arm and said, "Oh, yes there is!"

I handed it over and she took it out of the bag and saw the pink gift-wrapping from Goldsmith's. Exactly like I hoped, she could tell I was serious. She looked up and said, "Thank you very much, Elvis. This is such a pretty present." I knew right then I was in.

"Mama," Billie called inside to her mother, "come look at the present Elvis got me." Mrs. Rooker peeked her head into the hallway and saw me standing there. Mrs. Rooker was quick. She could tell right away what was happening.

"Why don't you invite your guest in," she said. "Don't make this young man wait out in the hall." We went inside to the living room.

"Should I open it now?" Billie said.

"Sure," I said, "no sense waiting till Christmas." Their apartment was very orderly and clean. The smell of baking cookies filled the room. Mother and daughter were close, I could see that right away. Mrs. Rooker took the present from Betty's hands and held it in her lap. "This is the prettiest present I've ever seen, darlin'. But you and Elvis hardly know each other." Mrs. Rooker looked at me; not in an unfriendly way, there was just a question in her eyes.

"That doesn't matter," I said. "You don't have to know somebody long to give them a present." I smiled at Mrs. Rooker, she knew my intentions were good.

Mrs. Rooker handed Billie the present. She unwrapped it and saw the jeans. "Elvis, you shouldn't of!" she hollered. "How'd you know I always wanted a pair of Levi's?" Her smile made me so happy. "This is my first pair," she said, "they're perfect. They're the right size, Momma, they'll fit perfect." She went over to the mirror and held 'em up in front of her. Mrs. Rooker nodded. I could tell she was trying to figure out what was gonna happen next.

We fell in love. Me more than her. We walked to school in the mornings and swapped stories about growing up in the country. There's so many characters to talk about when you've lived in small towns. We went to the little parties at the Courts, listened to music and slow danced, and played spin the bottle. I loved any game where the rules called for kissing all the girls!

We loved sitting out on the stoop and playing music. Billie'd relax and float away with me to wherever I wanted. She'd tilt her head back like a swan, her long hair touching the steps. She told me her dreams. She wanted to get married and stay in love. Billie's father had left when she was three, so she wanted something different for her children. She wanted somebody to really need her, just like I did. I taught her a few chords on the guitar. I'd always sung what I felt, but now there was somebody to sing my heart out to. We went steady for nearly two years.

When we had money, we'd go to the Suzores for a movie. Afterward we'd walk up Main Street and look in the shops, pointing at the things we liked, watching ourselves steal little kisses in the reflection of the windows. I'd never been in love before. Main Street was a glow of neon lights. I still remember glimpses of people we passed on the Street — the neon light made people seem timeless, like they were preserved in amber. We'd get to South Main and turn toward the river. There'd the Mississippi be in the moonlight, gleaming like tinfoil.

I remember one night, it was near the end, stopping at a park bench on the bluff above the Mississippi River. It was a warm summer evening. I said, "Do you ever wonder, Billie, where the Mississippi begins? Is it a little creek when it starts way up North? No matter how big something is, there's always a place where it starts." In the silver light of the moon the sea gulls made shadows on the shore. I wanted to tell her how much I loved her.

"I don't know, Elvis," she said, "the river's so wide I can't even see across it. I can't imagine the Mississippi ever being small." Billie thought me a dreamer, and I was. She said, "Do you ever wonder if there was something before creation? Is nothing something?"

I tickled her and she jumped. I was younger than Billie, emotionally I mean. She was ready to think about marriage and a family, and I was just a boy. I said, "Do you ever wonder if the moon's alive, Billie? I swear it's got a mind. I can feel it looking down on me some-times."

"What's it saying, Elvis?" Billie turned her head up to the moon and stars. I wanted to kiss all the little shadows the moon made on her face. I told Billie I loved her.

Billie brought her face close to mine. "You sure got pretty eyes, Elvis," she said, "too bad you're not a girl. Every girl in school would die for your eyelashes. They're so long."

"What's this, you're saying I oughta be a girl?" I joked with her, but I was disappointed she hadn't said she loved me back. It wasn't that she didn't love me. She did. It just wasn't as much for her, so she didn't want to say.

"No, silly, I'm not saying that," she said. "I want you to be a boy. A man. It's just that you're pretty enough to be a girl. Not all the time. But sometimes you are when the moon shines on you like this. Don't take it wrong. I love how handsome you are. You're just different from any boy I've known. It's like you got a million faces."

I turned her face back up to the moon, and whispered, "Have you ever floated up to it, Billie?"

She smiled and closed her eyes. "No, I can't say I have," she said.

I said, "You have to lose your weight and let your mind take you up."

"Can I do it with my eyes closed?" she laughed. It was a silly game to her, but I could do it, float up to the moon in my mind.

"Sure," I said, "imagine the moon's come inside you and that'll take you right up there. You can do the same with the river too, if you want." I knew in my bones that everything fit inside of everything else. I kissed her forehead and cheek, and the pretty line of her nose, with soft little kisses, following the shadows of the moon down her face.

We walked home hand in hand but our hearts were in different countries. I was thinking about us being together and having a life. Not that I had a plan, I was just a boy in love. Billie knew I wasn't the one for her — even if she thought I was great kisser — she wanted somebody older and more grown up.

Like most first loves, it ended in confusion. We broke up on a Friday night, in front of St. Mary's Church, across the street from the Courts. She went to a USO dance without me. I heard about it and went over to find out why. We stood underneath the lamp out front of the church. "I need to be free," she said. Her eyes were full of pain. It seemed unbelievable we were breaking up. But doesn't it always?

It Does What It Pleases

After I turned sixteen, that spring of '51, I started having nightmares. They were always at twilight in downtown Memphis amongst the brick buildings; guys were
chasing me and beating me up, they looked like Bowery
bums with stubbly beards and cigarettes rolled up in
their T-shirts, they were carrying chains and bats, the
whole nine yards. They'd get after me like heat-seeking
missiles, up fire escapes, down alleyways, crashing
through trash cans — with only one goal in mind — get
Elvis and beat the tar out of him. I was terrified and did-
n't even know why they were chasing me in the first
place. I'd run for awhile, then I'd fight 'em. Six at a time.
I'd wake-up in a sweat, the sheet wrapped around my
neck like I'd gone ten rounds with Rocky Marciano.

I wasn't any psychologist, but I knew enough to wonder what these dreams meant. It was hard to figure. I

had a few hassles at school, couple in the neighborhood, but I wasn't getting beat up or anything. I couldn't see any sense in these dreams, but they had a purpose: they'd come to make me stronger. You have to understand, I was a pretty meek kid. I was shy and I'd always been taught to be polite. I wasn't a mama's boy or a pansy, but I sure lacked confidence. I could disappear like a whisper and just blend into things. In some ways it was good. I was humble and respectful. But if you blinked you missed me.

You see I wasn't brought up to do what I did, that's where the nightmares came in. I needed more fight in me — not getting tough and beating people up, but the passion to be myself and go after what I wanted; otherwise you would've had Presley's Furniture Mart instead of "Hound Dog" or "Baby, Let's Play House." I had to blaze a new trail to be me. That's what the nightmares were for. They'd come to help me. I can see that now.

When these nightmares were done with me I wasn't the same. I was stronger, and better looking too. I'd gotten inside my own skin and taken over. There was a sparkle in my eye that hadn't been there before. I'd been born — and I was about ready to send out announcements.

Lemme tell you the dream that put an end to the nightmares. It was a real doozy. Came just in time too, man, the nightmares had about wore me out. In the dream I'm a pirate, the captain of one of those tall ships, the ones with sails as big as clouds. I'm about twenty years old and a real swashbuckler, kind of like Errol Flynn or Burt Lancaster.

The dream starts out with me on the deck of the ship. I'm having lots of fun with my pirate buddies, guys are climbing up the masts, swinging around on ropes with knives in their teeth, so it's a feisty scene. Then, these badass pirates come along our starboard in a schooner. They're really rasty with filthy beards and torn clothes, smelling of rum, and before we can do a thing about it, they jump aboard and capture us. They're gonna take us to an island and sell us into slavery — or maybe just kill us straight-out — we don't know.

The island comes into view, they unhook us from our chains and we pile into dinghies and row ashore. Near shore, we spot a herd of wild horses grazing on the headlands above the beach. The horses are gorgeous, they got broad chests and bristling muscles, every color from black to paint; they're bursting with energy and when they gallop their manes flow on the wind like Indian feather headdresses.

We pull the dinghies onto the beach looking up at the horses. I spot a white stallion who's leader of the herd. What an animal, he's got a long, dusty rose mane and sky-blue eyes. He's a prince of horses. Our eyes connect like you can with a horse sometimes. We know each other.

The stallion charges down the bluff with all his horses, raising a cloud of sand and dirt into the sky like a twister. Everybody's afraid we're gonna get trampled. The horses get down to the beach and pool up in a circle in front of us, the white stallion in the middle.

This is where the dream gets eerie. The horses begin to sing, but it's not like any song I've heard. They have incredible voices, not human voices — I mean they're horses — but they can really sing. The closest thing would be opera; it sounds like an aria or something. Their harmony's amazing, like the Mormon Tabernacle Choir; needless to say, this all has quite an impact on us pirates, the good guys and the bad; everybody — without an order or sign given — just drops to their knees, cause saint or sinner, we all know a miracle's going down.

My eyes are still locked on the white stallion's. I thought, this show is for me and my men. Just to make sure, I bow toward him. At this, he rises up on his hind legs and sings with even more power. His voice splits the world in two. I motion to my men to get the dinghies and head back into the surf. We do and the scoundrel pirates make no move to stop us. They understand that something higher has intervened. We walk away without a fight. As we row away the horses charge back up the cliff, take a turn around the headlands, and disappear like they've never been there at all.

I woke up feeling terrific. The trees and flowers out my bedroom window looked like they were waving for me to come outside and swim amongst them. I knew the divine had touched me, but it wasn't rapture like at church, it was a dream, and I didn't know what to make of that. I knew one thing though: God had touched me through the horses. I thought, the nightmares are over, and they were.

What I didn't know, though, was how the dream was offering me a path. My voice could carry the Spirit of wild horses, if that's what I chose.

e   *e*   *e*

"Elvis, it's time for you to get some sleep now, honey. You got school tomorrow." Momma'd say the same thing every night. I'd be in my room at the Courts playing the guitar, lost in music, listening to the radio or the record player. I had a little game I played, I pretended the voice on the record was coming from inside of me. And it was in a way; sound's so fluid, it moves so easy from here to there, it didn't take much imagining to transplant somebody else's voice into mine.

I liked every kind of music, Dean Martin and Eddy Arnold, the Ink Spots and Fats Domino; I played a lot of blues, Bill Broonzy and Big Boy Crudup, and rhythm and blues, Roy Brown and Lowell Fulson, Lloyd Price, B.B. King and Rufus Thomas. I had so many voices growing inside of me — I loved Hank Williams and I loved black gospel — Memphis had every kind of music. Later on I developed my own style, but in the beginning I tried on everybody.

I'd hear Momma hollering to me and glance at the clock. It'd be eleven and the last time I looked it was eight o'clock. I'd play a few more minutes, then put my guitar down so my parents could get some sleep. But I'd go on listening, turn the radio way down and put it next to my ear and fall asleep that way.

We had a group at the Courts, young bucks who thought we could play a little. Some of the guys were pretty good, like the Burnette Brothers who became rock 'n' roll stars themselves. Lee Denson was hot too. Johnny Black, the brother of Bill Black, my original bass player, played with us. We'd play at night underneath the magnolias out on the mall. The magnolia blossoms would mix with the warm breezes coming off the river. It was sweet, we'd make an entrance single file with our guitars and set up under the trees. People'd gather around, put down blankets on the grass or listen from their porches.

It was amateur hour but everybody had a good time. A few souls would get up and dance, inspired by the music or a couple of beers. We'd sing mostly country, "Tennessee Waltz" or "Cool Water," anything by Eddy Arnold was real popular. Folks at the Courts knew their country music, they were a good audience. They'd tell us, "You boys sound as good as the guys on the radio." We'd grin from ear to ear and swear we weren't.

Last thing I wanted was to take a solo. I'd sit in the back and disappear into rhythm and harmony. Didn't wanna be noticed cause I thought I was lousy. Indoors, I played in the dark. I'm serious. I wanted all the lights off! I was like a little kid, if you couldn't see me then you wouldn't know who was making the crummy music. People said they liked my voice, but I didn't believe them. I thought they were just trying to be nice. I wanted to be good. Music was the one thing I really cared about. I played and practiced all the time. It was funny, I thought I'd get good — that's what kept me practicing — but I never thought I *was* good, that was the carrot just out of my reach.

I was the worst when it came to having patience with music. Impatience can be deadly, though; a lot of people's problems boil down to a lack of patience. You can be on the right road and impatience will make you doubt yourself. Then you give up, when all you needed to do was keep on going.

People wonder where I got my look. Was it Brando or Tony Curtis, what'd James Dean have to do with it? as if I watched these guys and then pasted their look onto me. I don't think so. You can't take something from somebody else and stick it on, it's gotta come from the inside. Having style's not paging through a catalog of style stickers and gluing some on.

Lemme give 'em credit though, all those guys showed me how to *have* style. Put Liberace in there too, he showed me the fun side. You know where I learned a lot about style? Movies. Actors do intentionally what the rest of us do outta habit: Imagine a role and make a story of our lives. I almost got that while I was alive. It was on the tip of my tongue but I couldn't quite grasp it.

I got a job ushering at the Loew's State Theater on Main Street. I was sixteen. Did the whole thing — bell-hop uniform, flashlight, refused the hat, I looked too silly. It was one of those ritual jobs like guarding the queen of England. Wasn't much to do except stand there in the dark and watch the movie; that, or try to charm some candy from the girls at the candy counter. Which I was too good at actually. This other usher got jealous and snitched to the boss. Then I was real smart, I popped this bozo one, got fired, and had to go look for a real job.

But I ushered at Loew's State for over a year. I'd stand at back of the theater and watch the movies over and over and go into a trance like I was hypnotized. I never got bored. I'd finish up a shift and just sit down and keep watching. Saw all the great actors, Spencer Tracy, Humphrey Bogart, Katharine Hepburn, Robert Mitchum, all of them. Night after night, twenty-foot tall on the silver screen, they'd pour into my head. Same actors, different movies, over and over again. Had a big impact on me. I had a dream of myself, a way I wanted to be. These actors were doing it, people did it: they created themselves.

I started dressing kinda wild and let my hair grow long in a D.A., grew sideburns like the cross-country truckers I'd see on the Interstate. I got pretty wigged-out on clothes. I couldn't afford a lot, but what I had was colorful, yellow, green, and pink slacks (actually pink of everything I could get my hands on), shiny mohair sport coats in red, white, and baby blue, argyle socks with ties to match, and even those little jackets like bullfighters wear. I used to get stuff on layaway (dollar down, dollar a week). It was the "Hollywood" look, that's how Dewey Phillips advertised it on the radio for my favorite store, Lansky Brothers' on Beale Street. Actually it was the Beale Street look. I liked how the brothers dressed.

At times I looked weird even to me. I mean a bolero jacket and pink tuxedo stripes down your trousers will give you pause for thought. I wondered if I was flipping out; the kids at school thought so — maybe they were right! Basically I was a young white dude dressing like one of the men of Beale, and not cause I wanted to be black. I just liked the brothers' style better than the button-down look. The black dudes looked like they wanted to — they made themselves into a celebration if they were of a mind. And that's why I started getting my hair trimmed at a little black barber shop next to the Princess Theater too. The black barbers trimmed your hair how *you* wanted instead coming at you like a master sergeant with a lawnmower. It was a protest but I didn't care. I was gonna go to the beat of my own drummer and race be damned.

I was pretty schizophrenic in high school, one half of me couldn't wait to conform and the other coulda cared less what you thought about me — and I could do a flip-flop on you inside a minute too, no problem. I wanted to be normal like everybody else, and then I'd turn around and do something taboo like wear eye make-up, and not cause my sexual identity was confused, but just cause I felt like it.

Always was a contradiction this way, but in high school it was extreme. Wanted everybody to like me. Oh boy, did I ever want that, and if I thought you didn't, I'd go into overdrive trying to win you over. But if there was something I wanted to do, or needed to be, I was the most stubborn creature on God's green earth.

I kept having the same dream. I was a tightrope walker in a circus, up on a highwire. I was scared because I didn't know how to walk a highwire. But there I was, six stories up. I'd wake in a sweat, full of energy.

e   e   e

I loved the radio in high school, listening to Dewey Phillips or "KDIA" Memphis, the first black radio station in the country. There's an interesting story behind KDIA. Some white guys owned the station and they were going broke, this was in the late forties. As a last resort they decided to target the black audience, which may not sound like a stroke of marketing genius given the fact there were a couple of million African-Americans living within earshot of the station, not to mention Beale Street being two blocks away, but remember, these were Neanderthal times and a lot things about race didn't make much sense.

What the owners of "DIA" didn't count on, though, was all the white folks who wanted to hear the blues, race music as it was called then, and especially white teenagers like myself who were feeling a little rebellious to begin with. At Humes High School listening to KDIA got to be the underground thing to do. You weren't cool unless you knew all the disc jockeys and their hi-jinks. And if you really wanted to style, you cut class and cruised around with "DIA" on your car radio; so "DIA" became a huge success, I mean really big. Black radio stations and DJs started popping up all over the country. Even white guys got into the act, like Wolfman Jack down in Tijuana, Mexico. It's funny, you could tell things were changing before they did. Kids were lapping up rhythm and blues, cracking up with black DJs.

My favorite disc jockey, the biggest jive-master of 'em all, had to be Daddy "O" Dewey Phillips. What a piece of work he was: most eight-year-old boys grow up — Dewey never did — or more precisely, he never would, cause with Dewey you knew it was definitely a matter of choice. Dewey was a wildman and a speed freak, but he had a heart of gold. Our friendship went full circle. I started out idolizing him, then became a star and the roles reversed — we were good friends and then had a falling-out. The man loved me even though he drove me crazy.

Dewey had a voice like Pecos Bill's lasso; it'd grab you no matter what you were doing and pull you in. I first laid eyes on Dewey at Grants on Main Street, woulda been 1950, before Dewey became a disc jockey at WHBQ. I went into Grants to look at socks and Dewey was working in the record department. I'm just minding my own business, pawing through piles of socks, when Dewey comes over the squawk-box intercom like a bowling ball on fire. I remember he was talking up a new Hank Williams record. I'd never heard anybody talk so fast in my life. If mouths were cars, Dewey Phillips would of been a Ferrari Testarossa. He spit out a couple of chapters on Hank Williams inside twenty seconds, then he took off on the new Ink Spots record, and then it was on to Frankie Lane and Patti Page. My mind felt like a giant Ferris wheel.

I walked over to the record department to see the commotion. There was Dewey down on one knee on the record counter like Al Jolson, clutching a microphone to his mouth. His eyes were the size of ping-pong balls like those ol' time actors in the silent movies. Folks were crowding around him like kids to ice cream. Like all great salesmen, Dewey knew that most of all people wanna be entertained. Folks took money out of their wallets and purses and waved it front of his face. Dewey laughed that horsey laugh of his and grabbed up the money, passing out records as fast as a blackjack dealer.

Once he got his own radio show, Dewey owned Memphis. He was a crazy prophet; one listen to a song and Dewey could tell you its epicenter and magnitude. Nobody taught me more about music than Dewey

Phillips. He'd put something on, and if he didn't like it, he'd just pull it off thirty seconds into the record and say in that wry voice of his, "That don't cut it." Dewey was white, but he could imitate anybody — Fats Domino, Little Richard, Tennessee Ernie Ford, or Dizzy Dean. He didn't have a race, or an age; you could never place him.

He was wounded in the Korean War and got addicted to pain killers. He went from the narcotics to speed, and finally ended up taking the whole medicine cabinet to blot out his misery. At the end, he'd use the bathroom at Graceland and rifle through the cabinets for pills or a bottle of cough syrup. Dewey wasted a great talent, but that's what drugs will do to you.

He was on WHBQ six nights a week, nine to midnight; most nights I caught his show, that's how I learned music, practicing along with Dewey. He played everything — Como, Howlin' Wolf, Sinatra to Clyde McPhatter — and I played along, the great imposter copying everything I could learn.

I was big on rhythm and blues, and Dewey knew race music, the blues, as well as the Beale Street crowd. I'd always been around the blues but listening to Dewey is where I learned how to play 'em. Rhythm and blues is nothing but black gospel combined with the blues. Most rhythm and blues singers got their start in gospel, like Sam Cooke or Aretha Franklin. I liked the Platters and the Coasters, the Drifters, Elmore James, anybody who brought a beat to the blues.

Dewey Phillips felt the ground shake before any-body. There was a revolution coming and he heard it. He knew white folks wanted to hear the blues, race music, just as much as the blacks. God had a destiny for Memphis — it was a place for things to be mixed and joined — and Dewey was its Pied Piper.

Music's invisible, it goes where it wants and does what it pleases. The races were segregated when I was growing up, but music said, "No, I'll go where I want and do what I please." Music's an angel sent to earth to put things together that are supposed to be.

Pink Cadillac

Momma got a job as a nurse's aide at Saint Joseph's Hospital, around the corner from the Courts. She was good at it too. Folks were always giving her flowers, little gifts and thanks, for the help she'd been. The people at the hospital saw all this and wanted her to go to nursing school. She hadn't even gone to high school, so it would've taken Momma years to complete her course of studies. It was a honor just to be asked, though. I was so happy when she told me about the hospital's offer — finally other people saw how good she was.

It was at St. Joseph's, by the way, where the idea of the pink Cadillac got started. My momma came home one night from the hospital excited as could be about a car she'd seen. "I saw the most beautiful car in the world today," she said. "It was a Cadillac, pink, you shoulda seen it. It belongs to this nice lady from East Memphis.

Her son drove her over to the hospital in it."

"Did it have the wide whitewalls and white leather upholstery?" I was all ears. Cars were my fantasy.

"It had everything, and enough chrome to make a blind man see. I'd give anything for that car, Lord, it was the most beautiful thing on wheels you've ever seen. I gotta have one someday." All this and she didn't even drive, Daddy and me were her chauffeurs. It's not hard to see where I got my love of cars, my momma.

My Dad said, "All we gotta do is rob a bank, Gladys. Then we run over to the Cadillac dealer and buy it. Use it as a getaway car. We could do it as a family. What'd Machine Gun Kelly have that we don't?"

"I'm not gonna steal anything, Vernon." Momma could never resist Daddy's bait. "I'm gonna save up and get it. That's what I'll do." She sat down with paper and pencil and started figuring, that's how blitzed she was over this car. Didn't take long before she said, "It'll only take fifty years at two dollars a week, and that's not even counting interest." We all looked at each other and cracked up.

"You're gonna have a ball Gladys, tooling around the graveyard in your pink Cadillac." My Daddy had to take things to their outer limits. "Every ghost in Memphis will want a date."

"That's right, I'm gonna be the belle of the graveyard ball in my pink Cadillac. You'll be lucky to even get a ride." At least they could laugh together, that was always their saving grace.

Then I said, "I'm gonna buy you the car." They both looked at me and burst out laughing.

"And I'm the secretary of state. This here's the queen of England." Daddy thought I was joking.

I said it again, "I'm gonna buy you the car. I'll buy you a new pink Cadillac." Something in me knew I could do it. I stood with my hands on my hips, not even smiling, they could see I wasn't kidding. They stopped laughing and looked at each other puzzled as if to say, "The boy's crazy ... but what the heck, let's all be nuts together!" I didn't know myself where the confidence came from. I wanted so bad to give Momma something she wanted.

e   *e*   *e*

Momma and me were out running errands before Christmas, driving on Union, when she spotted a billboard out front of the Scottish Rite Temple. "I heard about this, Elvis," she said, pointing at their sign. "I think this is the place with the big pipe organ. I read about it in the newspaper."

"Should I stop?" I asked.

"Why don't you? Let's go take a look." We got out of the car and read the billboard in front of the building.

Momma said, "It says here it's Handel and Bach. The Messiah. I've heard it. It's very beautiful. This Sunday afternoon, a tea concert. We oughta go, Elvis." Her face lit up like a child's. "It'd be good for you to hear it, honey." I was surprised she wanted to go, usually she felt concerts like this were too highbrow. The job at St. Joseph's was giving her self-confidence.

I said, "OK, we oughta go." I liked classical music, just hadn't listened to it much. "We can ask Daddy if he wants to go." We both knew he probably wouldn't, but I kept wanting to ask him.

Momma borrowed some classical records from a neighbor at the Courts. We spent a couple of evenings listening to Chopin by Rubinstein and Debussy's Claire de Lune. Mario Lanza too. I couldn't believe the man's control and vibrato. Opera could of been a passion for me.

Momma and me went. We got all dressed up for our tea concert. It was a gigantic pipe organ in an upstairs music room of the temple. Some of the reeds were the size of tree trunks. The room was pretty small so it felt like God was playing it, the whole room rumbled and your body shook on the low notes. I was awe-struck. I thought, God has brought me to the concert to hear the power of His music in a whole new way. I'll never forget the look on Momma's face as she listened. She was an angel in a masterpiece painting.

Afterwards we went downtown to eat, to the grill at the Peabody Hotel. I'd always wanted to go but it was too expensive. Momma was in a great mood and she insisted. "I've always wanted to go there too, honey. We're dressed for it, it'll be my treat."

They sat us down at a table next to a window. It was cold outside and the heat of the dining room fogged over the windows. The glasses and silverware, the white linen tablecloth, it was all so beautiful. The concert, and then a fine restaurant, it felt like we'd stepped into somebody else's life. The grill was out front where you could see it; the chefs in high hats were carefully placing hamburgers and mounds of hash browns and bacon on the grill as little wisps of smoke rose around their heads toward a glass case filled with pies. The place was packed and people were waiting for tables.

"It was heaven, Elvis, wasn't it the most wonderful thing you ever heard? You know who would've loved it was your Uncle Noah. He's the classical music lover in the family." It was nearly Christmas and people bustled past our window in the dark loaded down with packages. "That Bach, or however you pronounce him, that music was like a stairway I was climbing, Elvis. I went higher and higher until I disappeared."

"I know," I said, "it was from God, like gospel music. I'd give anything to be able to play like that, bring people that kinda joy."

"You can honey. You don't know how good you are. God has a plan for you. You just gotta trust you can do it, that's all that stands in your way." It wasn't anything different from what she always said. Nobody ever believed in me as much as my mother.

"I hope so, it's what I want more than anything, playing music. I guess we'll see pretty soon. How about you? What do you want? You're always helping me, but what about you?"

"I don't know, honey. I'm worried." She didn't look afraid. She was concentrating. "I've prayed on it but no answer comes. I'm not happy and don't know what to do."

"What is it? Is there something I can do? Is it money?"

"No, money's not it. It's always a problem, but that's not it. It's about what I wanna do. I want to be a nurse. I thought it was silly, take me as long as getting that fool Cadillac. But it wouldn't really."

"What do you mean? How could you do it?"

"I could study and take tests to graduate from high school. Wouldn't have to go class every day for years. Then I could go on to nursing school and keep working at the hospital. There's nurses there who've done it."

"Well, why not then? What's the problem?"

"It's your daddy. I don't think he could stand me doing it. I asked him about it and he just joked me, said I could finish nursing school same time I got my pink Cadillac.

Then he said we could have a perpetual Presley at Humes High, that is after I finished the eighth grade at Christine School. He didn't wanna take it serious. You know how he is when he don't wanna touch something."

"You could do it anyway. He can't stop you, nobody can."

"I don't know, Elvis, be awful hard. After all these years going back to school, I think I'd have to do it on my own. Without your daddy."

She stunned me. She complained about my dad for years, said maybe we'd be better off on our own, but this was different. She wasn't in a mood. She was clear as a bell.

The Hardings

My Dad and me got on some funny riffs sometimes. I remember one Saturday waxing the car with him. We were listening to a World Series game on the car radio, the New York Yankees and the Brooklyn Dodgers. I was a Dodger fan cause the Yankees won all the time. Daddy loved the Yankees from the time of Babe Ruth and Lou Gehrig; Joe Dimaggio, the Yankee Clipper, was his favorite. This day, like always, he polished the Ford coupe like Michelangelo. He'd do two-foot squares of the car, meticulously rubbing in the wax, and buff it with a Turkish towel. Then he'd go over the same square to cherry-it-out. My Dad was a flat-out perfectionist if he cared about something. He just didn't care about a whole lot of things.

Our natures were different that way. I always needed to be pumped-up about something. Daddy, on the other hand, didn't have any guiding passions. It just wasn't his nature to take a tack with something and stay with it, although he was a fanatic when it came to detail. He could of been a great finish carpenter. We were an odd pair, all I cared about was the big picture and he only focused on details. It was nobody's fault, we just didn't quite match.

We were at the Courts on Winchester, across the street from the ghetto. We lived near, or in, the ghetto for many years, both in Tupelo and Memphis; so for those of you who wonder if I heard black music growing up, it was so routine I didn't even give it a thought. Some black kids were jamming across the street. The sound of the blues and a ballgame on the car radio, I loved the streets of Memphis.

Daddy and me joked back and forth as we shined the car. He was wearing a grey porkpie hat pushed back on his head like Jimmy Durante. For a change it didn't seem like we were trying with each other. We got along OK — that wasn't the problem — it just seemed like we were always starting from square one. How can you live with somebody for forty years and still feel like you're a stranger? I never could figure it out, although I tried. I wondered if it had to do with him going to jail for a year, to Parchman Farm, when I was three years old.

It was a fool prank that put him in the joint. He and a couple of buddies got swindled on a hog deal by a skin-flint businessman in East Tupelo named Orville Bean.

They took matters into their own hands and forged Bean's check to even things. It was a kid prank more than anything, but Bean decided to make an example of them. He refused restitution, and they were sentenced to three years in the state penitentiary, although Daddy got out after a year for good behavior. This was 1938.

Talk about a scary time, Momma thought we were gonna starve to death ... at night she was frightened of the trees outside the house. She'd shake so bad I had to put a blanket over her. Every other Sunday we'd take the bus over to Parchman to visit my dad. We'd leave Tupelo before sunrise and ride the bus for five hours. It was *so* weird. I'd see Daddy for maybe a half-hour, then he and Momma would go off and I'd play in the back yard of the warden's house with a bunch of kids. No one ever explained to me what in the world was going on — for all I knew he'd taken an axe to somebody instead of the chump-change they'd put him away for. We had to get to know each other all over again after he got out of prison.

Across the street, the young brothers were singing rhythm and blues, Roy Brown's "Good Rockin' Tonight." I bopped along to the music and sang as I polished the front grill and hood. My dad looked up from the trunk. He winked and said, "You could go over and join them, Elvis. I don't know, son, you're starting to sound like them."

I laughed. There was nothing racial in his comment. Daddy wasn't a hater. He got on good with black folks. I said, "I'm fixing to conk my hair, Daddy, get it slicked down clean." Me and my cousin Gene had a fantasy of getting our hair conked.

Daddy said, pointing across the street, "You do that and you're moving over there." As he spoke, the black kids who'd been playing the music walked across the street with an older gentleman. The older guy was about Daddy's age. He came up to Dad and said, "You wouldn't be Vernon Presley from Tupelo, would you, sir?"

Daddy pushed his hat back on his head and said, "Yes. I'm Vernon Presley. We live here now." He pointed over to the Courts. "But I'm from Tupelo," he said, "where would I have known you?" There was nerves in his voice, he felt a little wary.

I figured the older gentleman was the kids' father. He looked like he loaded ship for a living, his forearms were the size of ripe pineapples. The boys stood a couple of feet behind their dad holding on to the necks of their guitars. I smiled and nodded hello; they broke into grins and nodded back.

The father spoke, he was wearing tan work clothes and work boots. "Mr. Presley, I don't think you'd remember me, sir, but you helped me once and I've never forgotten it. The boys were playing outside today and I noticed you and your son waxing your car." He nodded toward me. "It was your hat, Mr. Presley, that's how I knew you, sir. You were wearing the same hat the night you helped me." He gestured with his hands and shook his head, laughing as he spoke. He was a lively guy, a real bright spirit. I figured he was probably a man of God.

Daddy scratched the side of his head. "You need to refresh my memory, I'm afraid, I can't quite place you." Daddy was smiling too, you couldn't help but like this guy.

"It was late one night, Mr. Presley, in Shakerag." Shakerag was the black ghetto in Tupelo. "I was in a terrible fix. My brother needed me out in the county. His daughter was deathly ill and had to be brought into town to the hospital. My truck had a flat tire and I'd lent out my spare."

"Yeah. I remember now," Daddy said, "that was quite awhile ago. We were living over on Mulberry Alley by the Fairgrounds. I remember you. But I'm sorry, sir, I forgot your name." I went around to the trunk of the car and stood beside my dad.

"Warren. Warren Harding, Mr. Presley. These here are my sons, Gerald and Demetrius." The boys and me shook hands all around. They were about my age. "You gave me the spare tire off your Ford truck, Mr. Presley, and I've never forgotten your kindness. You can ask the boys. I don't know what would've happened to my niece if I hadn't got her to the doctor's that night. She had a terrific fever, 104 degrees by the time we got her to the hospital. They got penicillin into her and she was fine."

Daddy said, "You said you had a sick relative. You got the spare back the next morning, I remember that. It was in the back of my truck." Mr. Harding and the boys smiled.

I pointed at Gerald and Demetrius's guitars and said, "I play a little too." Gerald offered me his guitar but I was too embarrassed. They'd sounded pretty good across the street and I didn't wanna come off as a rank amateur. Gerald was the oldest, he was tall and muscular with a long neck and deep-set eyes. He stood there with his arms crossed and Demetrius, who was squat and stocky, stood on one foot and leaned back against his brother's chest. Demetrius laughed out loud, his cheeks looked like a squirrel's. The boys were checking me out, I was wearing a chartreuse Hollywood shirt and lightning bolt slacks. A white boy looking like a Beale Street hipster, it was hard for Gerald and Demetrius to figure.

Mr. Harding and Daddy talked about Tupelo. Turned out we'd been neighbors there too. "Mr. Presley," Warren said, "I'd like to give you a little something, if you'd accept it, sir, on account of how kind you've been to our family. I gotta say, it's a small world, ain't it, us being neighbors again. It's the Lord's will, I guess, for us to be meeting. I would've never recognized you except for that hat, Mr. Presley." He paused for a moment, and then he said, "I have some mirrors I make, with mosaic tiles, and it would be my pleasure for you and your family to have one of them."

"There's no need for that, Warren. Don't be giving me nothing," Daddy said. "You telling me your niece is OK is thanks enough."

"You all come over. We got ice-cold tea, and beer, whatever you want, and I'll give you one of my mirrors." Warren was a proud man, but you could see in his eyes he wondered if we'd come to his house.

Daddy looked at me. "Elvis," he asked, "you wanna take a break?"

I was curious what these mirrors with the mosaic tiles looked like. "Sure," I said, and I put my wax and towels on the front seat of the car.

The five of us crossed the street and went over to the Harding's place. They lived in the bottom floor of a big house that'd been split up into two apartments. Their porch was nice, the boys had their guitar picks and bot- tlenecks laying out on a table in front of an old swing. A pair of bongo drums was sitting underneath the table.

"Which one of you all, Gerald or Demetrius, plays the drums?" I asked.

Demetrius spoke. He had a deep voice. "Gerald and me can't play 'em. Their my Dad's. He says he learned shipping out to the Caribbean Islands."

Warren said, "Gerald, why don't you take Mr. Presley and Elvis around back to the shop and I'll get us some refreshments."

We walked around the side of the house past beautiful beds of yellow and pink roses. Mr. Harding's workshop was in the garage. He had it fixed up like a den. There was a couch and stools and a counter he used as a wet bar. All his tools were shined and neatly put away. A couple of posters from the Palace Theater on Beale Street were on the wall behind the counter.

Mr. Harding came through the door with a tray of drinks and passed them around. Everybody got settled and Warren said, "Mr. Presley, when you all come upcountry to Memphis? Florence and I, my wife, came up with the boys two years ago. My brother, the same one you helped, got me on at the Sanitation Department with him. We even on the same truck now."

"It was '49, nearabout," Daddy said. "I worked in Memphis during the war. Man's got more opportunity in the city. You got a chance to move up. Elvis here is gonna get a trade. There's plenty of work, even though the war's over."

Gerald, Demetrius, and me were sitting on the stools at the wet bar. Gerald took a pad and pen from a drawer at the bottom of the counter and drew a tic-tac-toe game. He put an "X" in the upper left hand square. "You play?" he asked, and he put the paper and pen in front of me. I smiled and marked an "O" in the middle square. Demetrius lay over the counter and played cars with the drink coasters and watched Gerald and me. He had the same kind of thick arms as his daddy.

"Myself, I wonders if the war is over." Warren said. "The Red Chinese they spoiling for a fight. Korea's just the tip of the iceberg. Although I hope it doesn't come to them fighting. I'd hate to see it."

We boys looked at each other but didn't say anything. The Korean War never seemed real. It wasn't like the Second World War.

Daddy said, "You fight in the war, Warren?"

"Yes, sir. I did," he said. "Paratroopers. Italy and then France." I tried to imagine Warren in his soldier's uniform. You didn't think about blacks as soldiers fighting and dying for America, but they sure did.

There was a pause in Daddy and Warren's conversation, and then Warren said, "Mr. Vernon, would you like to see my mirrors? They're in there," he pointed to a door on the side wall. "Come on, we'll take a look and see which mirror matches your home furnishings."

I thought the shop was just one room, but Warren opened what looked like a closet door and it was a work room with no windows. In the middle of the room was a dining-room table. Mosaic tiles and pieces of mirror and strips of metal were scattered on top of it. On the walls of the room were Mr. Harding's mirrors. Round mirrors, and sunbursts, and a few triangle-shaped ones. Modern-looking stuff, they reminded me of things I'd seen in magazines. They were handsome mirrors. Daddy liked them too; he went over to the far wall, stepping around the dining-room table, and admired a round sunburst mirror with yellow and orange tiles. Gerald and Demetrius sat down at the table and started working on mirrors they were making.

Daddy walked around the room looking at Warren's mirrors. Then he lingered in front of the orange and yellow sunburst. It was always hard for my father to say what he wanted.

"Is that the one you take a liking to, Mr. Vernon?" Warren asked. "You all take anything you see, now. All these are yours."

"This one," Daddy said, pointing to the orange and yellow sunburst. "I'd be mighty proud to have it." He looked back at Warren through the mirror.

Mr. Harding carefully packed the mirror in a cardboard box with crushed newspapers. "I wondered who'd get this one." Warren said. "Goes to show you, life's a mystery. It ended up being Vernon Presley's!"

We all laughed.

We said goodbye to the Hardings and went back to the car and finished waxing it. Daddy and me decided to go to town for a snack. We walked down Poplar as the sun was getting low over the river. You can't see the river from there, but I always knew where it was. I said to my dad, "I betcha I can eat more doughnuts than you."

"I don't think so," he says. "I outweigh you by forty pounds. It's a stupid bet anyway, we'd only make ourselves sick." But the idea of an eating contest had grabbed his mind, he was cracking up, smacking his lips like a chimpanzee. "It's a bet I can't afford to win or lose," he says. "I'm paying, ain't I?"

I sure didn't have any money. I said, "You're just scared I'll eat more doughnuts than you, and I can." I knew how to get my dad. He didn't like to lose at anything, even something stupid like eating doughnuts.

"Where you gonna put these doughnuts, Elvis," he said, "in that hollow leg your momma swears we're feeding?" He grabbed me as we walked along and rubbed a noogie on top of my head. He made me laugh so hard I got the hiccups. I loved it when Daddy let loose. He said, "I don't think I should do it to you, son, half-dozen doughnuts and you'll be screaming for castor oil. It's not right for a father to do." He tried to keep a straight face but his eyes crinkled up like an elf's.

I said, "You're scared, that's all, you know I can out-eat you."

He had a couple extra bucks so we had our doughnut-eating contest. I beat him by a mile, he was done after four chocolate doughnuts. He said it was over, no more, but I figured the winner had the right to keep on eating. We settled on seven glazed doughnuts, and I was happy.

The Minstrel Show

The Humes talent show, the annual Spring Minstrel Show at school, was coming up and I was trying to decide whether or not to enter it. "The talent contest is coming up at school," I said to my cousin, Gene Smith, as we sipped our Purple Cows. Gene worked at Hall's Grocery on Mississippi Boulevard and ran their dairy bar in the afternoon. "Mrs. Scrivener announced it in class. It's in April. I'm fixing to do it, I think. I gotta sign up this month. I thought about it last year, but then I chickened out." I was a senior and this would be my last chance to enter the contest.

Gene took a long drink of his Purple Cow, set it down on the counter, and said, "I remember."

"You remember what?"

"I remember you talking about it. You were scared then and you still are. But Lord knows I'd pee in my pants if I tried to get up in front of an audience full of people and sing. I gotta hand it to you, buddy, for even trying."

You never had to worry about where you stood with Gene, he'd tell you to your face. He was too blunt actually, it got him into trouble, but Gene'd give you the shirt off his back. The boy loved cars and speed, and anything wearing a skirt.

"So what do you think. Should I do it, Gene?" Gene was the closest thing I had to a brother. We were the same age and raised up together. Point of fact, Gene was seven weeks older than me and he never let me forget it; he was always reminding me that he was the older and wiser one, deserving of respect.

"It don't matter if you win, Elvis. I know ... you think I'm just throwing you a bone to make you feel better. The thing of it is, you're a singer so you ought to sing. There's no choice about it. If you don't sing you'll feel like a coward, and you'll always wonder how you would've done. Then you'll be like the rest of the grown-ups, full of regrets." Gene picked up the glasses and plates sitting on the counter and washed 'em in the sink. He looked like a choirboy, fine blond hair and blue eyes, but Gene was a triphammer — you didn't wanna cross him, I'll tell you that. He mighta been skinny, about 145 pounds dripping wet, but he had a pair of guns on him and he was quick as a fox.

He looked at me in the mirror in front of him and said, "If you don't do it you'll fail before you even start. It's all in the mind, that where the battle is." He went back to carefully washing each dish in the sink. "You wanna another Purple Cow, Elvis?" Purple Cows were our favorites, Nugrape soda pop floats with vanilla ice cream.

"I know," I said, "it's just postponing things not to do it. As long as the Purple Cows are free, Gene, I'll keep drinking."

"You don't know how good you are, Elvis. When you find out — when *you* believe it — then your break will come."

I listened. Gene knew all about struggle. He'd grown up a sharecropper, in Shannon, about ten miles south of Tupelo at a plantation named White Spot. There might of been a hundred folks in Shannon if you counted the dogs. Gene went to school when his family could spare him from the fields. The school was in Verona, in an old railroad car, all the grades were in the one room. There was no quit in Gene, he was a fighter. I was lucky to still be in school, having a chance to enter a talent contest. I looked in Gene's eyes in the mirror, he was thinking the same thing.

Gene took a big scoop of vanilla ice cream from a ten gallon tub, lifted it above his shoulder with the flourish of an orchestra conductor, dropped the ice cream into a frosty glass and poured in the Nugrape from high above, without spilling a drop.

e   *e*   *e*

It wasn't just for myself that I wanted success — I wanted to help my mom and dad, my whole family for that matter. We'd been poor forever. It was like a disease. We weren't hungry and we had the clothes on our backs, but that was about it. My mom and dad were only in their thirties, but they were already growing old and tired. We were on the bottom looking up — no money, no savings — just hard jobs that went nowhere. But the bottom's not such a bad place; from there, if you dig a little deeper, you can get to essentials.

All I had was my faith. I prayed to God to guide me. And my prayers went deep. It's obvious what happened: God came to me through music. I believed in miracles, healings, speaking in tongues, prophecies, sanctifications, and gifts of the Spirit. That's how I was raised. Some of you may have judgments about this — you may put it down as mumbo jumbo — but it's my truth. I became a man on bended knee. It's how I found the strength. I prayed for a healing of me and my family.

I told my homeroom teacher, Miss Scrivener, that I wanted to sign up for the Humes Minstrel Show. She smiled at me and said, "I know you're gonna do very well, Elvis Presley." I told her I hoped so.

"**I** hear you're going out for the Minstrel Show, Elvis." I was at Charlie's Record Shop talking with Johnny Black, the little brother of Bill Black, my future bass player.

"Who told you that?" I said.

"Red West. He said he was gonna do it and you were too. Told me last week."

"I signed up so I reckon I got to. Don't know what to play though. I'd like to play some blues but that'd probably freak everybody out. Come out and sing 'Dust My Broom' or 'Rocket Eighty-Eight.' Maybe 'Boogie Woogie Woman.' It'd be all these barbershop quartets and marching music, and there I'd be singing low-down blues." I noticed Charlie Hazelgrove, the owner of the store, had gone behind the counter and was shuffling through records deciding what to put on next. I said, "Charlie, how 'bout putting some 'Boogie Woogie Woman' on?" and went back to my conversation with Johnny.

"Why don't you give 'em some race music, Elvis," Johnny said. "It's a minstrel show, you could do the whole thing in blackface."

"Yeah. Right. Maybe I should conk my hair and wear a zoot suit too. Everybody thinks I'm weird already, Johnny. That'd just prove it." Charlie Hazelgrove put "Boogie Woogie Woman" on the record player.

"So what do you think you'll sing, Elvis? Some Eddy Arnold?"

"I don't think so. Hank Williams maybe. I gotta think about the audience, what folks'll like."

Charlie Hazelgrove hollered over to us, "You boys heard 'The Bearcat' yet, Rufus Thomas' new song? Ol' Rufus sounds like a mountain lion, like he been starving out in the Ozarks all winter. Says it's his answer to 'Hound Dog.'" Charlie put "Bearcat" on. Rufus Thomas did sound like a wildcat. It was amazing.

I said to Johnny, "I just don't wanna get up there in front of everybody and be tongue-tied."

"Everybody feels that way at first, Elvis," Johnny said. "It's just how it goes. Then you learn to relax and it's easy. Think about everybody in the audience sitting on a toilet. That's what works for me." He laughed.

"Good idea, man," I said, "why didn't I think of that? How 'bout you becoming my manager? Maybe we could both wear toilet seats over our heads."

"There you go, now, you're catching the spirit. It just don't matter. You gotta keep that in mind, first and foremost." Johnny looked out the window at the traffic on Main Street. He headed for the door and stood out on the sidewalk. Cars were bumper to bumper in the rush hour traffic. I watched him through the window. He made faces and stuck out his tongue at passing cars, jumping up and down on one leg like a pogo stick. He looked like a rodeo clown. Johnny was crazy, but this was far-gone, man. I knocked on the window but he did-n't hear me. I was about to tell Charlie Hazelgrove to come have a look, then I reckoned he might get ticked-off at Johnny for making a scene in front of his store. Johnny turned around and stuck out his tongue at me and burst out laughing. Then he came back inside.

"See?" he said. "Nobody even noticed me. Might as well have some fun. Nobody notices anything anyhow. I coulda worn a toilet seat out there."

e *e* *e*

I couldn't decide on what to sing for the talent show. I wanted to do "Boogie Woogie Woman," the B.B. King hit, but I didn't have the guts. I thought about a couple of country songs, "Keep Them Cold Icy Fingers Off Of Me" and my old standby, "Old Shep." That's what I sung at the Mississippi-Alabama Fair when I was a kid. I was learn-ing Teresa Brewer's new song, too, "Til I Waltz Again With You." I figured a country song would go over best with the audience. It'd give people something they knew.

I didn't get a chance to practice for the talent show like I wanted cause we had to move out of the Courts. We were making too much money. What a joke, but rules were rules, so we had to go. That was OK. It was time for us to try our wings anyhow. We moved to a rooming house on Saffrans for a month, and then found a house, a downstairs apartment, right across from the Courts on Alabama Street. I went back to work at Loew's State to help pay the rent.

I was too busy to get in much practice time for the talent show.

The Minstrel Show was on a Thursday night. This was the beginning of April, 1953. They got my name wrong on the program, spelled it Elvis Prestly. I didn't care, if I screwed up maybe people would think it was somebody else. Fat chance. Everybody knew me and thought I was weird. My parents really wanted to go and see me perform, particularly my mother. I wasn't that hot on the idea, but it would've killed her not to come.

It was hilarious getting ready for the show. I musta combed my hair for an hour and a half. Three different kinds of pomade, one for the fall, one for the D.A., and then Brylcreem on the sides. I couldn't find the right shirt so I borrowed one from Bobby Ford — bright red flannel with white buttons — I wanted to stand out and reckoned a red shirt would do the trick. Then, wouldn't you know it, I tore a hole in the sleeve hanging it up in the closet. I just rolled the sleeves up and decided to dedicate the song to Bobby, that way he couldn't get mad at me.

Night of the show, backstage was like a menagerie. Every different kind of act was getting ready. There was a xylophone trio, a marching band, a cute-as-a-button five-year-old girl twirling a baton, acrobats, and tap-dancers. Red West was warming up on trumpet.

Miss Scrivener had us come early cause there wasn't gonna be any rehearsal. She clapped her hands and gathered us around. "People," she said, "we're all gonna come out together at the beginning for a grand opening. The school band's gonna play 'Camp Town Races' and then the curtain'll come up. So you gotta be out on stage and ready to go and not in the bathroom or talking to your friends. And we got a lot of performers this evening, like I expected. It's come out to be thirty. So everybody's gonna have just one song. Whoever wins — and that's gonna be decided by the applause from the audience — gets to come back out for an encore. You all wish each other luck now and do your best. Remember, all the folks out there wanna see you do well."

I stood at the edge of the stage at a crack in the curtain, that way I could see the audience and whoever was on. The place was packed to the balconies with moms and dads, brothers and sisters. I recognized a lot of people. My stomach churned like a taffy pull, which's where I always felt the stress, in my stomach. The Humes Auditorium was new then, probably had seating for six hundred people or more. I was used to little parties at the Courts, or singing for a few stray firemen at the fire-house, but a crowd this big freaked me out.

I wanted people to like me so bad. After all is said and done it boiled down to just that — wanting people to like me. Love me really. That never changed. The feeling was always the same.

The truth comes to the surface no matter how big or famous you are. Many years later (getting ready for some shows at the Astrodome in Houston) I felt the same as this first night back in Memphis. It was in 1970, I'd just started touring again and I was afraid the venue was too big. I'd never be able to fill up a 60,000 seat stadium. The first show, a Friday afternoon, only sixteen thousand people came, and a lot of those were comps. I went back to the Astroworld Hotel, across the street from the Dome, down in the dumps. I mean really depressed. I figured that was it, I'd lost the magic. I didn't care about the money, or even the fame, I just wanted people to love me. I needed it, although I didn't wanna admit that to anybody, and least of all to myself. I dragged myself up to my room and sat on the bed and prayed. Then I took a nap.

After dark my cousin Gee Gee Gambill came into the room and opened the curtains. He said, "Elvis, come look." I got up and went to the windows. Lines of car lights stretched for miles out onto the highways around the Astrodome. Gee Gee left the room and I put my head down on the table and cried like a baby.

The little baton girl was up first. Helen was her name. She looked like a miniature cheerleader for the Tennessee Volunteers. That's the music she chose too, the Volunteers' fight-song. She pranced from one end of the stage to the other, her blond ponytail bouncing to the music. Never took her eyes off the audience except to toss her baton high in the air. She brought the house down. I thought, this little girl's gonna be tough competition.

The acts kept coming, barbershop quartets, the xylophone trio, a pretty girl playing accordion. I was up after the Humes Band, they did "Beautiful Ohio." I was standing offstage holding my guitar waiting for my name to be announced. It was and I froze, couldn't move a muscle. Finally somebody said, "Elvis, you're on, get on out there." It was like I was sleepwalking or in a dream.

There was a chair center stage. I put my leg up and swung my guitar in front. I stood for a second amazed like I was seeing the world for the first time. I planned on doing "Old Shep," but then I changed my mind, right on the spot, and decided to do "Keep Those Cold Icy Fingers Off Of Me." It was a sixth sense, I knew the audience would like "Icy Fingers" better. I remembered to dedicate it to Bobby Ford, and without further ado, I began.

It felt like somebody else was singing the song, like I was watching myself. The song was coming out fine so my attention went to the crowd. Peoples' faces and their eyes. This was the first time I felt how much an audience wants a performer to do well. There's a yearning inside of folks to be lifted to higher ground. I wanted to give the crowd everything I had.

I got done and worried for a second I'd left something out. But then the applause broke loose. They liked me, they really liked my singing. It was the most wonderful feeling.

I got off stage and Miss Scrivener was waiting for me. I saw the light in her eyes too. I said, "Miss Scrivener, they like me, they really like me."

She said, "Yes they did, Elvis Presley. They liked you very much. Don't you go far now." I was shocked she thought I might win.

And then I did. I went back out for an encore, did Teresa Brewer's song "Til I Waltz Again With You." It was the number one hit and I knew the crowd would love it.

e   *e*   *e*

After the Minstrel Show things were different at school. I wasn't weird no more, I had a little talent, so now I was eccentric. It was a relief not to be just plain weird! I started bringing my guitar to school like I'd done in Tupelo and playing at lunchtime. It gave me a bridge to people, a way to get to know them. The kids had thought I was stuck-up cause of how I dressed and my hair, now they could see I was the same as everybody else.

The end of the year we had our Senior Picnic at Overton Park. I rode on the bus next to Georgia Avergis, a friend of mine from the Courts. "How do you like your new house, Elvis?" she said. "I haven't seen you around much." Georgia was a beautiful brunette with eyes as deep as the sea.

"I like it fine," I said. "I'm only across the street, Georgia, it's not like I moved across town." We were just friends because her religion didn't allow her to date anybody who wasn't Greek. I really liked her and her family. I'll tell you this, Georgia's mother was the best cook — the smell of Mrs. Avergis's homemade bread turned me into one of Pavlov's dogs.

Georgia said, "It's different though. I don't see you anymore. Oh, I did you see playing football the other day at the triangle. I missed the Minstrel Show. Everybody said you were wonderful. The girls have been talking about you, but I guess you know that."

"Oh yeah. What they been saying? Probably talking about how strange I am, like from another planet."

"You know that's not true. You just like to talk on this way. Girls are interested in you but you're always keeping to yourself." Georgia was a pistol, when she got excited her cheeks would turn rosy-pink. "You don't give people a chance to know you, although there's girls who'd like to, I'll tell you that. There's one sitting up in front of this bus right now."

"What are you getting started Georgia? You wanna see me make a fool of myself, like that guy in the Shakespeare play we read who goes around wearing the head of an ass."

"Oh no, you like her too. I can tell."

"Who you talking about?"

"Carolyn Poole, that's who."

"You're nutcake, Georgia. Carolyn Poole wouldn't take a second look at me. She's got too much money."

"That's where you're wrong, Elvis Presley. You think you know so much but you don't know the nose on your face."

The bus stopped in front of the Overton Park Shell. Everybody walked across the street to the picnic tables, but I strolled inside the amphitheater with my guitar. I walked up the side of the bowl to the last bench and sat down. The sun was halfway up the morning sky. The Overton Shell's just benches on lawn, but it has a deep feeling about it like it's ancient.

For years I'd hitchhiked over to the Shell to hear concerts, sat in the cheap seats outside the amphitheater under the spreading elms and oaks. I was always amazed by the classical musicians and how they could play piece after piece and never look at a sheet of music. I closed my eyes and imagined myself on stage with everybody watching. Then I opened my eyes and looked around at the empty benches. Not a soul was there but me. I prayed for my dream to come true.

Mr. Sam

Sun Records was just a little place off Union next to Miss Taylor's diner. Everybody at Sun hung out at Miss Taylor's, it was like the front room of the studio. Sun was something special even before it got famous. A white guy, Sam Phillips, was recording race music, the blues, crossing over black music with white. That got peoples' attention. This was the early fifties and the separation of the races was the rule. All the brothers on Beale Street knew about Sam Phillips and Sun Records. In the pawn-shops, in Beale Park, everybody had a jive story about going over to Sun and making a record.

After I got outta high school, I'll tell you, Sun was my burning bush. I went to that mountain with a lump in my throat. My dream was to make a hit record at Sun. I was greener than grass. What do they call it — your salad days? — well, in that case I was a jumbo tostado. I drove by Sun for months before I got up the guts to go in. My old Lincoln Zephyr knew the way over there by itself.

It was incredible what Sam did with that little rig of his on Union. It was such an itty-bitty place, but boy, if ever a mouse roared, Sun was it. Jerry Lee Lewis came out of Sun Records, Carl Perkins and B.B. King, Johnny Cash, Roy Orbison, Charlie Rich.

Miss Taylor's was sort of a Memphis version of that drugstore in Hollywood, Schwab's, where people went to see stars or get themselves discovered. A lot of blues people, B.B. King, Roscoe Gordon, Bobby "Blue" Bland, were in and out Miss Taylor's on their way to Sun. That first time I went into Miss Taylor's, man was I nervous — combed my hair for ten minutes in the rearview mirror of the car before I got up the courage to walk across the street — I didn't know whether to skip or yodel.

Soon as I walked through the door I saw Sam Phillips sitting in a booth by the window. I knew him from his picture in the paper. There'd been an article about a prison group he'd recorded, the Prisonaires, from the Tennessee State Penitentiary. The record was "Just Walking In The Rain" and it became a hit. You might of heard Johnny Ray's cover of it a few years later, that was an even bigger hit.

I sat down at the counter and it felt like everybody in Miss Taylor's was looking at me. Nobody was paying me any mind, but when you're young and needy it feels like the eyes of the world are on you. The waitress at the counter got me a peach soda and then asked if I wanted a hamburger. She was a redhead, a blue-eyed buxom flirt named Cindy.

I ordered a cheeseburger and peeked over at Sam Phillips without being too obvious. "Will that be with or without?" Cindy asked. I didn't know what she was referring to. Didn't have a chance to answer before she said, "Now, darlin, there's always time for fries." She sucked on the end of her pencil and smiled at me like a Siamese cat. Her hair was short in a bob like a pixie's. "You look like a fella who wants it 'with.'" She turned her cute backside to me and flipped a burger through a cloud of smoke and landed it, plop! on the grill.

I could tell Sam Phillips was smart from his eyes. Some people drink in the world with their eyes like the high tide of a flood. His had that hungry look. He was sitting in the booth with two guys, one white and the other black. I didn't recognize the black gentleman but I figured he was probably a musician of some sort. The white guy was Jack Clement, a country singer I'd seen around. Sam was better looking than his picture in the paper. He was tall as a blade and handsome like a young Gregory Peck. Sharp dresser too. I never saw Sam Phillips with his shoes unshined or without a crease in his trousers. The man had purpose no matter what he did.

Funny, I always thought about how me and Sam were different. But I know the truth under the skin now, and how we're the same is more important. I was afraid of being weak, same as Sam, which's where our stubborn-ness came from.

e   *e*   *e*

I watched Sam with his friends in the booth. He used his hands to talk, tilted his head to one side and then the other. Sam smiled and asked questions with his eyes. He reminded me of the Italian grocers on Main Street showing off their fruit to customers. It was about five-thirty and Miss Taylor's was filling up with people getting off work. This was before integration and the civil rights marches, and I wasn't used to seeing whites and blacks together in a diner.

Cindy was finishing up my cheeseburger, wrapping paper around it and setting it on a plate. She brought it over. "Are you a musician, a recording star or something?"

I said, "What are you talking about?"

"I think I saw your picture on a poster for a show. I betcha that's what you do. You're a musician of some sort."

"You didn't see my picture unless you were looking at one of my dreams. I want to be a musician. I'm just getting started, trying to find somebody who needs a singer. How 'bout you. Where'd you go to school?"

"I didn't go to school in Memphis. I just moved from Little Rock." She introduced herself and asked my name.

"Elvis? What kind of name is that?"

"It's a family name, I suppose. Nobody knows how it got started. Don't have to worry about getting confused with anybody."

"Elvis Presley," she repeated. "That's true."

I knew she'd go out with me if I asked her.

Sam and his friends got up to go. He turned and looked right at me, half raised his hand like he knew me. Then he put it back down and went on out the door.

I wanted something from Sam Phillips real bad: his approval. I thought maybe I'd get discovered. There wasn't a reason on God's green earth why I should of been. I hadn't done anything. But I always thought anything was possible. Besides, if you wanna catch a train you gotta go to the station. So that's what I did.

Sun

You could go into Sun Records and make a recording for four bucks. Sam Phillips did the recording himself. I figured it was a cheap audition, and I'd give the record to my mom for a present.

The day was hot enough to fry eggs on the hood of your car. I was practicing out on the porch at Alabama Street when it hit me that I should go over to Sun, right then, and make the record. I threw on a pair of slacks and a white shirt, grabbed my little Gene Autry guitar, and was walking through the door of Sun Records inside ten minutes. If I'd thought about it I'd a been lost.

Actually it wasn't called Sun Records, its name was something else. The Memphis Recording Service. The whole front of the place was closed down with venetian blinds to keep out the sun. I cracked up, no sun at Sun. I peeked in Miss Taylor's and Cindy waved at me to come inside. I waved back but didn't go in. She looked darn good but the last thing I needed was distractions. I stepped inside and there was Marion Keisker sitting at this big desk in the foyer. I liked her from the get-go. The woman was an angel.

Marion gave me this wonderful smile. "Good afternoon, how can I help you?" she said. She had the eyes of a deer and fine features like a piece of sculpture. The room was white and a ceiling fan cut the air like the oars of a boat.

"Good afternoon, ma'am," I said. "How are you today?" She was in a baby blue summer dress and her blond hair curled over her shoulders. "I'd like to make a record, please. You wouldn't know anybody who might need a singer, ma'am?" I just said the first thing that popped into my head. I could never plan out what to say — it screwed things up. I'd stutter or get stuff backwards — weird things would come out — it was better if I didn't think.

Wooden chairs lined the walls for people waiting to make records. Most days the chairs were full, but this particular afternoon there wasn't anybody else there. Marion motioned for me to sit down in the chair beside her desk. She took out a piece of paper. "What's your name, sir?"

"Elvis Presley, ma'am. I live here in Memphis." She reminded me of a beautiful bird, her arms and legs were graceful as a swan's. I figured she was in her early thirties.

"E-L-V-I-S, is that how you spell it?" She wrote my name down. I was sitting beside her maybe two or three feet away. Her handwriting was beautiful. There was a sunburst clock above her head and I remember it was ten past three. She asked me, "What kind of singer are you?"

I said, "I sing all kinds."

Then she said, "Who do you sound like?"

I told her, "I don't sound like nobody."

"Well you gotta sound like somebody," she said. She had spunk, Marion Keisker. Had her own radio show for years in Memphis. Marion was one of the first lady talk show hosts anywhere, U.S. or otherwise.

"Do you sing hillbilly?"

I thought about her question. Figured she pegged me as a hillbilly singer cause of my Mississippi accent. I heard car tires bumping over the hot streets outside.

"I can sing hillbilly, ma'am, but I'm not a hillbilly singer."

"You sing hillbilly, but you're not a hillbilly singer." She laughed and covered her mouth. I hadn't said any-thing funny. Then she asked me, "Do you sing pop music? "

"I can sing pop, ma'am, but I'm not a pop singer."

Marion laughed right out loud at that. I didn't know what was so funny. I sang hillbilly and pop music, but I wasn't just that. Then Miss Keisker said, "You can sing hillbilly and pop, but that's not what you are. You don't sound like nobody else?" She was trying to figure me out. My long hair and sideburns made me look a little tough I guess.

"Sure," I said, "I can sing all kinds of music. I don't reckon I sound like nobody else though."

I wasn't trying to be difficult, but I didn't get the joke. She thought I was saying I was an original — that there was nobody else like me — which I wasn't saying at all. All I was saying was I didn't sound hillbilly or pop or any of just one thing. But she thought I was telling her I was an original talent, which I never would have had the guts to say. I was saying one thing and she was understanding something else.

It was always like this for me, though, I can't tell you how many times it happened and I just flowed with it. I mean what's the point of contradicting somebody if they're liking you? Might as well let it ride. But there was something else going on too. When you say the right thing without knowing why, could be you're getting help.

Marion said, "So you'd like to make a record, Mr. Presley." I nodded and said that's why I'd come. She gave me a few directions on what to do and led me through the door into the studio. It was different from what I expected. I guess my idea of a studio came from looking at pictures in magazines, you know — guys in bow ties standing around boom mikes with women on their tippy toes. This was more like a warehouse, except not as big; there were those tiles with the little holes, walls and ceiling. I noticed an upright piano and a drum set, some standup mikes, and lots of wires running everywhere. Sam Phillips was behind a big window on the far wall. He was fiddling with some equipment. I figured he was mixing a record or something.

He looked up and came over to the doorway of the control room to greet me. He didn't remember me from Miss Taylor's. He'd just had an argument with his partner and he looked nervous. He was brusque with me, but I expected it. Sam Phillips was a busy man. I just wanted to get on with it anyhow. Besides, what was I gonna say, except maybe drop to my knees and beg him to like me. Marion helped me get set up and Sam went back inside the control room.

Mr. Phillips gave me the sign to get started. I opened my mouth and it felt like somebody'd stuffed a watermelon down my throat. This bad voice in my head crackled like a down wire, "This is it. You gotta do it. Don't mess up." Finally I calmed down and launched into "My Happiness," a song I'd been practicing for about a year. "My Happiness" is a real gentle song with warm flows like the Hawaiian ocean. It's funny with a song, sometimes it's the music and sometimes it's the lyrics that touch your soul. With "My Happiness" it was the lyrics, although I didn't know it at the time. But that's how it is with lyrics, they travel inside us and find homes in our souls. That's why a lyric can pop into your head outta the blue sometimes and exactly describe what you're feeling.

"My Happiness" is a lonely song. It talks about missing somebody for a million years. I think the record came out pretty good considering how young I was. I was eighteen. The song has a solitary feel like my voice is floating all alone in eternity. I always felt sad with the song, not in a bad way, but the way a blues song can cut you open. What I didn't get, though, was how the lyrics had found a home in the story of my life. They were touching the soul in me that knew, even then, that my mother was gonna die.

I got done singing and looked up at Sam Phillips in the control booth. This was the first time a professional had heard me sing and I couldn't wait to see his reaction. Of course you know what happened with all this build-up: He didn't have much of a reaction at all. He looked at me kinda puzzled and said, "That's good, son, you put some feeling in it. What are you gonna do for the other side?" He didn't know how to place me. That made sense. I didn't know how to place me either.

We recorded a "B" side for the record. I did "That's Where Your Heartache Begins." Didn't come out as good as "My Happiness." It was stiffer, more mechanical, and I didn't feel it as deep. Mr. Sam didn't have much of a reaction to it either, all he said was "OK, we got your record." He came out and stood in the doorway to say goodbye. Offhand, he said I was an interesting singer and he'd keep me in mind. I searched his eyes and then walked away. I felt pretty good. He hadn't decided anything against me. He knew I was around and that was a start.

I went back out to Marion's office. She was making up a label for my record on the typewriter. She motioned for me to sit down and I watched her fingers move over the keys. She took the label out of the typewriter and carefully glued it on my record. I was attracted to her, but she was too old for me. She belonged with a lawyer, or a doctor, somebody from City Hall. I didn't figure she'd be interested in anybody like me. As I was set to leave, I asked if I could check back with her, see if anybody might need a singer. "Please do," she said. I felt my stomach quake. She was gonna help me, I knew it.

I stayed in touch with Marion. Whenever I'd stop in at Miss Taylor's, I'd poke my head inside Sun and say hello. It got to be a joke between us. She'd gimme a little smile and say she could never forget Elvis Presley. And she didn't. It was her nudging Sam Phillips that finally got him to call me back. If it hadn't been for Marion Keisker, I'd a been lost in the shuffle.

After I started recording with Sun, Marion and I became good friends. She handled publicity so we went out on interviews together. If I didn't know the answer to something, she did.

e   *e*   *e*

I'm mustering out of the Army in Germany, this was 1960, and who do I run into but Marion Keisker. I kid you not. She was a captain in the Air Force stationed in Europe working for Armed Forces TV. Sam and her had a blow-up and she joined the service. She was lonely and full of disappointment at this point in her life but you never would of guessed it. Like old times, she was there to encourage me. And I'll tell you, I needed it. I didn't know if things'd be the same after two years in the Army. I thought my career might be in the dumpster. Marion pumped up my confidence this day, even wagged her finger in my face.

I was flabbergasted we'd run in to each other halfway around the world. "Everybody misses you," she said. "It's gonna be better than ever, Elvis." Even then I realized God had sent her to me.

You know God has a sense of humor. He gives us little teasers through the veil if we know what to look for. I had this odd thought over the years about Marion that kept rolling around my head. Every time I'd see her the thought, "Medieval French," would pop into my brain. That's what Marion studied in college, Medieval French. I never asked her about it, somebody else had told me. It was just a strange thought, "Medieval French," that'd rattle around my head when I'd see her. It struck me as funny; I'd chuckle a little bit to myself and go about my business.

I didn't know anything about French — not old, new,

or future — but it was a clue as to who Marion was. Marion Keisker had been an angel in Renaissance times; that's why the thought kept coming to me.

East Trigg

I was always taught to keep it simple, if you needed money any job was OK: better to make a dollar an hour than sit on your can. The summer I graduated from Humes I worked at Parker Machine, then in the fall I went back to Precision Tool, with my cousin, Gene. Precision Tool was in the armament business. They made 105 millimeter shells for the Army — big, whomping bullets! — Gene and me worked the day shift, seven a.m. to three-thirty.

Walking into Precision Tool, you'd a thought you'd arrived at hell, it was like a witches' coven, your nose stung from the boiling chemicals and the assembly line belched smoke and made such a racket you had to scream to be heard. The shells were dipped in one stinky vat after another, and then they were put on the assembly line where we stood and scoured them clean. You had to work fast or you'd lose all the skin off your hands. We made a buck twenty-five an hour and the work was tougher than nails, but we couldn't find anything better.

Factory workers — the folks who work our assembly lines — are our unsung heroes as far as I'm concerned; takes all a person's got, sometimes including their health. Professionals talk about stress and burnout, well, somebody ought stand up for the working stiff who lays it all down and has to keep his mouth shut. Later, when I got to thinking concert tours were rough, all I'd have to do to cure my burnout was remember working at Precision Tool.

Most of the family worked at Precision Tool at one time or another. It came to tragedy, too; my cousin Robert, Gene's brother, was fatally injured in '69 at Precision Tool; it was called Diamond Plating then. Robert fell in a vat of boiling chemicals and was severely burned. For a month he struggled for life in a burn unit. People make so much of what I went through and what happened to me, but there's good folks everywhere struggling against much deeper odds than I ever bucked.

Gene and me worked side by side on the assembly line, hollering at each other like two madmen above the noise. We had a secret language that was pretty hilarious — we dreamed it up in high school after seeing a cowboys and Indians movie (we cut our wrists and pledged undying brotherhood) — after that, we needed a secret language for our private communications when other people were around, so we talked backwards to each other, the last word of a sentence coming first, and to really throw people a curve, we sang certain words so people'd think we were trying to remember the lyrics to a song! It was pretty stupid, for example, if we wanted to say, "we are blood brothers" it would come out, "brothers blood are we!" People didn't know what to think.

Both of us wanted more for our lives than Precision Tool. There was no future there or way to get ahead. I needed to help my mom and dad, that was uppermost in my mind. If I had a chance it was with the music. I felt bad for Gene, he didn't really have a way out. I prayed for guidance and swore I'd help Gene if things worked out.

e   *e*   *e*

"Oh man," I said, "I wish this zit would go away." Me and Gene were driving over to K's Drive-in; we were gonna grab some hamburgers and then go to a black church, East Trigg Baptist, for their Sunday night Camp Meeting.

Gene watched me looking at myself in the rear view mirror and said, "Somebody oughta invent a zit-cream that works, he'd make a million dollars, the first day.

Say, look at that Fleetwood." A Cadillac Fleetwood, bad and black, passed us on the right. "Probably a crook or a politician — or both! What time does this Camp Meeting get started, Elvis?"

"It starts at seven," I said, "that's when the radio broadcast begins."

It was the "Camp Meeting of the Air," a black gospel hour with Reverend Brewster on WHBQ. I'd listened to the show for a couple of years over the radio and enjoyed it, and now I was taking them up on their invitation to come by and see the services in person.

The traffic light turned red and I pumped the brake pedal. The brakes on the Lincoln were shot, steel on steel, so me and Gene opened the doors and slowed the car down to a halt with our feet. We looked like a couple of Keystone Kops, it was pretty hilarious.

The car came to a stop, the brake drums screaming for mercy. "We had any brains, Elvis," Gene said, "we'd figure out it was cheaper getting this clunker brakes than us buying new shoe leather."

"That's true," I laughed, "particularly these two-tone jobs, I'll be buying another pair on lay-away before these are paid off." I was styling in black slacks with a pink jacket and green shirt, all lay-away specials from Lansky Brothers'. Gene was in Lansky's finest too, a black mohair jacket with a chartreuse shirt and mother-of-pearl cuff links. We had our shirt collars flipped-up under our hair for that Hollywood look.

I said, "What do you think the black folks at East Trigg will think of us? They'll probably wonder why a couple of white boys are dressing like Beale Street. Or maybe they'll be dressed the same."

"I don't think so, Elvis," Gene said. "Oh, maybe a few of the women will have feathers on, but these are church folks, not the Beale Street crowd. This'll be a whole different class of people — upright, Christian — besides if they went to Beale last night they've had the day to recover."

"You're probably right," I said, "hope they don't think we're rank sinners."

"If they do," Gene said picking some lint off his jacket, "at least they'll be glad we're at church."

We got to K's Drive-in and I saw Cindy, the waitress from Miss Taylor's, across the street, leaning up against a car at Earl's Hot Biscuits. "Hey, let's go to Earl's," I said, "there's that Cindy girl I was telling you about from Miss Taylor's."

"Not b-b-bad, b-b-brother-blood," Gene said. "You could do a lot worse — and you have!" Gene slugged me on the shoulder and grinned.

"Yeah, she's nice too." We pulled into Earl's and parked a few stalls away from Cindy and her friends. Cindy saw us though, she gave us a big wave as we docked the Lincoln.

"Here she comes, Elvis, with one of her friends."

"Well, if it's not Elvis Presley," Cindy said, leaning

down to my window. "That's a name I'll never forget." She and her friend burst out laughing and covered their faces. Her friend was tall and blond, elegant like one of those Afghan purebreds.

I said, "What trouble you girls up to now? Who's your friend, Cindy?" Cindy was wearing bright red lipstick and she had a big smirk on her face. Her friend was leaning over trying to catch a peek at Gene.

"This here's Ellen, Ellen Hughes, she's my next door neighbor," Cindy said.

"This is my cousin, Gene Smith," I said. "We're on our way over to the East Trigg Camp Meeting."

Gene said hello to the girls. "You two could be sisters," he said. He leaned over me, his arm draped around the steering wheel. I didn't see the resemblance, but Gene was just trying to make a few points with them. "Say, have you two eaten already?" He smiled, turning on the charm.

Cindy said, "No, we just got here and ran into some friends."

Gene said, "Well, why don't you all climb in the back seat and we'll order some hamburgers and shakes."

I opened the door and got out and the girls climbed in. My guitar was lying on the back seat and Cindy slid it over. I thought, things are clicking tonight, we been in Earl's five minutes and we got a couple of pretty girls sitting in our back seat.

"This here's your guitar, Elvis?" Cindy asked. She was chewing bubble gum and popped a big one all over her luscious lips.

Ellen chimed in, "Cindy said you're a musician, Elvis, a singer. You all a musician too, Gene?" Ellen had a sparkle in her eye. She was Gene's type, too, long and sleek.

"No, I can't say that I am," he said. "Elvis got all the musician genes in the family. They all done lined-up and marched into the boy. He's really good, I'm not kidding, Elvis can flat-out play."

"Would you play for us, Elvis?" Cindy said. She was holding my guitar between her legs, draped over it like an acoustic bass. "Please," she said, batting her eyes. She reached over and put her hand on my shoulder. Gene looked down, trying not to laugh. He knew it didn't take much of an invite for me to play.

"OK," I said, "I guess I could. Why don't we order our stuff first, then I'll play till it comes."

We ordered our cheeseburgers and shakes, and Gene said, "Let's get out of the car. Elvis can't play the guitar in here."

I strapped on my guitar and leaned up against the front fender. I just started "Boogie Woogie Woman," the B.B. King song, when a friend of mine, Luke North, walked up with a friend. They'd just driven into Earl's and saw me playing. I smiled at Luke and kept on. *"I got*

*a boogie woogie woman and she boogies all the time ...
if she keeps on boogeying she's bound to lose her mind."*
Luke North, who was a good drummer in his own right,
took a pencil out of his pocket and beat out a rhythm
line on the hood of the Lincoln. A little crowd gathered
around us to listen. Everybody was digging the song and
boogeying a little themselves. *"She boogies in the morning and she boogies all night long, when the morning
comes she's still boogeying strong."*

People loved the song, but that was no surprise. I
knew from experience that folks took to the race music,
the blues, best cause it made them feel good. I was surprised to see Luke North. I thought he was away at
school.

"Luke," I said, "I thought you were at Ole Miss. You
couldn't of flunked-out this soon, buddy." Luke had
started his first semester at Ole Miss down at Oxford,
Mississippi.

"Hey, boy, looks like you all having a great time," Luke
said. "I'm just up for the weekend to get some more of
my stuff. I'll be heading back tonight. This here is my
friend, Bobby, from school. Bobby was dark and stocky
with a short crew cut. He had on a sport coat like the
college guys wear with the leather patches on the
elbows.

I introduced Luke to everybody. "You all, Cindy, Ellen,
this is Luke North, an old friend of mine from the Courts.
Luke here is the best drummer around, although the

boy's real calling ought to be the law — on account of Luke's slippery tongue. Lemme tell you about the time me and Luke played hooky from school and went to Wolf River. This was in eleventh grade, we took the Jackson bus all the way out there. Had a great ol' time.

"Next day at school, me and Luke caught it — we had to pay a visit to Mr. Brindley's office, the principal. Brindley comes out and takes a look at the two of us sitting on his bench and says, 'Which one of you wants to come in first?' I said, 'Lemme go on in and get it over with, Mr. Brindley.' Brindley talks to me for a minute and then he tells me to bend over. He takes his wooden paddle down from the wall and whacks me, hard, three times. I apologized for cutting school and swore I'd never do it again. I walked out of there like I'd spent all night in the saddle.

"Then Luke goes in for his turn. Mr. Brindley says to him, 'What am I suppose to see you about, young man?'

"Luke says, this is all with a straight face mind you, 'Should I take my English class, Mr. Brindley, during summer school or wait for my senior year?' Brindley tells him not to worry about it. Take the class his senior year. And that's it. He don't get no paddling.

"Afterwards, Luke runs up to me at my locker in the hallway, smiling like he just pulled off a Brink's robbery, and tells me what happened with Mr. Brindley. I'll tell you, I was about ready to whip Luke's butt on the spot myself."

"You gotta look innocent, Elvis," Luke laughed, "no matter how guilty you are. Brindley was probably all worn out from swatting you anyhow, didn't have another paddling in him." Everybody laughed.

"Elvis and Gene, what's this camp meeting you all going to tonight?" Cindy said.

I said, "It's Reverend Brewster's Church, East Trigg Baptist, in South town. It's been on the radio for awhile, the music's out of this world. You all heard of Queen C. Anderson, she's one of the best black gospel singers in the country."

"Oh, it's a Negro church," Cindy said, "that does sound exciting. I know the colored folks really raise the roof in their meetings. This is the first time you've gone, huh?"

Gene and I said, "Yeah."

Then Luke's friend, Bobby, said, "Whatcha all doing going to a nigger church?" Everybody got quiet, but he went on. "Don't see as how *their* church is any business of ours." He looked at everybody with the question in his eyes, expecting people to back him up. Cindy and Ellen looked away, and Luke just stared at Bobby.

Gene said, "I guess, Bobby, you did say your name was Bobby, right ... I guess, Bobby, it don't seem to me like it's any business of yours what Elvis and me decide to do tonight." He said it real polite and slow, enunciating every word. The veins in Bobby's neck bulged out. Gene was at a low-boil, I'd seen his anger build many times;

one sideways word out of Bobby and Gene'd put him flat on his back.

I snapped — I don't know if it was seeing Gene get angry or what. "You got a problem with me and Gene going to a black church, Bobby?" I said. I was ready to take him right there.

Luke put his hand on my shoulder. "Cool off, Elvis," he said, "we don't wanna fight here. Everybody's got a right to their opinion."

Bobby said, "I guess I'm not used to things here in Memphis. It's not like *this* where I come from." He said it with a sneer, like Memphis was beneath him. I didn't even think about it, I slugged Bobby in the face and knocked him to the ground.

Gene stood over Bobby and said, "Better stay down for awhile, sport, if you know what's good for you." Bobby rubbed his face and didn't get up. The girls were scared. They walked away with their heads down and their arms around each other.

Luke was breathing hard. He said, "That's it. You guys knock it off. Or I'll finish the both of you." I felt bad. There's better ways than fists. I wanted to apologize to Luke but I didn't.

I said, "You shouldn't of pushed me, Bobby." Bobby glared but didn't say anything. I felt like an idiot. What was I gonna do, fight every redneck in the South, good luck.

Gene came over and took my guitar. "Come on," he said, "let's get out here, Elvis." We drove off. Cindy called to me as we drove away. I rolled down the window and said I'd talk to her at Miss Taylor's. We jammed out Mississippi Boulevard, I had my foot to the floor.

e   *e*   *e*

I was all jumbled-up as we tried to find Reverend Brewster's Church. I had the address on a piece of paper, thought it was in my pocket, but it'd fallen out at Earl's. We drove East Trigg slow and finally found the church on the right-hand side, 1185 East Trigg. The sign out front read: East Trigg Missionary Baptist, Reverend W. Herbert Brewster.

It was a white clapboard building, two-stories and neat as a pin, Reverend Brewster's house was next door. People were walking up the flight of stairs to the entrance of the church. I saw other white people going in, so we wouldn't be the only ones. It was bigger inside than it looked. One of the ushers, a dignified black gentleman with a white carnation in his lapel, directed Gene and me upstairs where the visitors sat. The inside of the church was nothing fancy, dark wood with wooden pews. They had it set up like a stage, there was a sound engineer for the radio broadcast and stage lights ran on a beam above the pulpit.

We got there just in time, the Brewsteraires, the church chorus, was already lined up. I'd never seen Reverend Brewster, but I didn't have any trouble spotting him from the balcony. He stood out like a prince, tall and upright as a tree in good soil. He was beautifully dressed in a tailored, dark blue suit with French cuffs and silver cuff links. His face was long and kind, and with his glasses, he looked like an ambassador or a head of state.

He stepped to the pulpit and smiled at the congregation for a good, long moment before he said a word. I looked over at Gene. He winked and said, "This guy's the real thing, man." Gene and me had a great view, center of the balcony in the first row. Reverend Brewster held our souls in the radiance of his smile and then he began. "We are moving to higher ground, ladies and gentlemen. Can you feel God lift us? Can you feel Him move us up? There *is* a new day coming when all men will know their brotherhood. God has a plan for us, and it is not the trough of hatred or the wallow of prejudice."

I was still feeling upset over Bobby. I thought, did I do the right thing hitting him? He was surprised, I saw it on his face. Two wrongs don't make a right, though, but what else could I of done?

"We have a special treat for you all this evening," Reverend Brewster's voice was deep and resonant, "and for all the listeners on the radio. Mr. Gatemouth Moore, one of the great entertainers of our time, has recently come to the Lord. He is here with us this evening to share his stirring voice and inspired wisdom. Before all that, though, let's use our voices to clear our souls, and feel, ladies and gentlemen, the lift of our Lord, Jesus Christ, as He moves on up, higher!"

Queen C. Anderson was alone at a microphone to Reverend Brewster's right, she answered his *"higher"* with one of her own. *"Higher,"* she sang, *"Higher, higher."* She had the voice of a songbird inside that big body of hers. It helps being stout, just plain big, if you wanna sing with the kind of power she had. The piano player found the downbeat of "Move On Up a Little Higher." Reverend Brewster raised his arms joyously and the congregation rose. Chills washed over me.

I looked at Gene, he was singing with his eyes closed. Queen C. answered our lines with, *"Higher, Moving up Higher"* — she had perfect rhythm, perfect beat. Her timing was flawless. I looked around at all the black people and thought: they ain't all one color, they're orange and coffee, and chocolate. It don't make sense to think they're the same either. God sees everybody the same though. The coloreds put more feeling into His music than anybody, I thought.

I wondered how Bobby was and if Luke would stay mad at me.

Reverend Brewster, who'd been standing by Queen C.

as she sang, moved back to the pulpit. I looked at Queen and saw the light of her soul, then I talked myself out of it. We see with our hearts for a minute, then our minds say no. "Ladies and gentlemen," Reverend Brewster said, "if I were to recount to you all the accomplishments of our guest this evening, Mr. Dwight 'Gatemouth' Moore, we would have time for little else.

"Instead, let me tell you the amazing story of how Gatemouth Moore found God. Those of you acquainted with blues music know that Gatemouth Moore is the greatest blues singer of our generation. At the height of his career, four years ago, in 1949, he was touched by the Lord in an unlikely place. But, as we all know, there is no mountain tall enough or valley so low for the Spirit of Jesus to miss us. In the great city of Chicago, at the famous Club DeLisa (this was in the cold of winter nineteen and forty-nine) Gatemouth Moore went on stage as the featured entertainer of the evening. He stepped up to the microphone amidst the wealth and finery of that elegant club, but ladies and gentlemen, nothing came out of his mouth. He tried again ... but, once again, nothing came out. The next time Dwight Moore made the effort, the spiritual "Shine on Me" came forth from him spontaneously; sisters and brothers, Gatemouth Moore sang the words of the Lord, without benefit of his mind or reason!"

I been good friends with some blacks, I thought, it just never took. Like John Allen Cooke. He looked for me every day in Tupelo; if I missed a day delivering for Brown's Grocery he and Curtis Johnson drove around looking for me. They drove all the way out into the fields to find me. I couldn't tell them we were friends, though, and they couldn't tell me. I didn't tell anybody. You're suppose to keep it secret how you feel about black folks.

Reverend Brewster finished up his introduction of Gatemouth, and Gatemouth ambled up to the pulpit with a big smile. He used a walking stick with a gold-plated handle, swinging his other arm out wide with the Bible in it. He didn't need the cane, it was there just for style.

"Thank you all for your kind applause," Gatemouth began. "I hope I can hit the mark for you all this evening. I know Jesus can, He sees the bull's-eye of Spirit deep in our souls." Gatemouth looked up toward heaven and smiled, his mouth full of gold. "Trying to hit the mark," he laughed ... "it reminds me of a funny story. It seems one morning there was these two hens, young pullets, strolling across the yard when they spots a cross-eyed rooster checking 'em both out. The one pullet turns to the other and says, 'Honey, you and I had best separate, because if we don't, he liable to miss us both!'"

The congregation burst out laughing. They have a lot more fun at their church than we do, I thought. People couldn't take their eyes off Gatemouth. They're wrapped in mystery, these black folks, they're too smart for whites to solve.

Gatemouth stepped in front of the pulpit and raised his hands to the ceiling, drinking in the congregation like a Roman conqueror. *"Shine on Me, Lord, Shine on Me."* He began to sing the song God smote him with at that club in Chicago. Reverend Brewster motioned for us all to join hands. I clasped Gene's hand. A middle-aged black woman was on my other side. She looked like a school teacher, proper and upright. She waited for me to give my hand. I did and she smiled from her heart. We sang the refrain, *"Shine on Me ... Shine on Me ... Shine on Me,"* and swayed back and forth like one big chain.

It was a whirlwind, the timbers of that ol' church shook like a three-day fever. Queen C. and Gatemouth Moore broke out the tambourines. It was like those tent meetings of the Black Sanctified Church I used to go to in Tupelo, behind our house on North Green Street. There'd always be a few of us white kids standing at the back of the tent listening. It was a game of cat and mouse with those black preachers then. They'd start off slow, whispering and sweet-talking you, then they'd take it up, moving and shaking, asking people to get up and testify. When everybody was all worked up, they'd start pleading: Give yourself to Jesus! People'd be crying, getting slain of the Spirit. The chorus and piano'd go higher and higher. What a party!

Queen C. sang slow on the other side of the stage across from Gatemouth, her face filling with light like an angel's. The congregation joined arms. Reverend

Brewster stepped to the mike and raised his arms above his head. "Brothers and sister," he said, "take this Spirit of Jesus with you into the world. Carry Him in your hearts. You *know* the truth is His love and joy. Carry Jesus' love as your shield and sword. He is the light shining forth beneath all your troubles."

Gene and me hung around after the service and talked to everybody out front. Black folks, their passion and mystery is so deep.

Green Beetle

I got off work early from Precision Tool, and came home in the middle of the day. Momma was still in her housecoat and slippers, sitting on the front room couch. She looked depressed. "You been crying," I said, "your eyes are red." I knew it was about my dad. She had a whole mood about her that went along with being upset with him.

"I got the blues, I guess," she said, "sometimes I feel like walking into the Mississippi." I hated it when she got depressed like this. I didn't know what to do.

"What happened?" I said. "You and Daddy had another argument, huh?"

She said, "I don't know what's what anymore, Elvis. As fast as I pedal, I stay in the same place. And all I do is eat and get fat." She leaned over slow for her cigarettes, her back was acting up again.

"What's he gone and done now?" I said.

"I can't talk about it," she said.

"You just don't wanna tell me what happened, Momma."

"Your daddy got in late last night, again." She only needed a little prompting to tell everything. "He said he lost track of time over at the Green Beetle. 'There's nothing wrong, it's all in your head, Gladys,' he says, 'we was playing pool and drinking beer and nobody looked at the clock. Give a man a break.'

"I don't know if I should believe him. It's always one excuse or another. Next thing he'll tell me, the stuffed deer's climbed down from the wall of the Green Beetle and kidnapped 'em all." She laughed and slammed her pack of cigarettes down on the coffee table. She had a sense of humor even when she was messed up.

"What are you gonna do?" I said.

I knew how the whole scene went, nobody was gonna snitch on my dad. She wouldn't know what was going on with him.

"It's nothing for you to worry over, Elvis," she said, "you got enough worry going to work every morning. I'm so proud of you, graduating from high school. Now you got a good job. You're a man already, Elvis. You don't need to be thinking about your daddy and me." She had a heart of gold, my mother. Every chance she got she built me up.

I said, "You think Daddy's going out. I already know it."

She was gonna be all right, this kind of thing happened between them. "Well, listen to you, Mr. Dumbo Ears," she said, "you been listening to everything, haven't you?"

"I heard you all arguing last night. Sounded like you both been drinking." They drank too much, that was part of their problem.

"I can't speak for your daddy, but I had a couple of glasses of beer here at home. That's it, as God is my witness."

She always made excuses about alcohol. "I ain't accusing you of nothing," I said. I had enough sense to know I couldn't do anything about their drinking.

"So, you already know everything, huh?" She looked at me trying to guess what I knew. "I think your daddy's stepping out on me. There's just been too many late nights and excuses. I know your daddy — since he was seventeen — your father can't pull the wool over my eyes. He's got the same itch as your Grandpa Dee, although he ain't mean with it like Dee was. Maybe that's the problem, Vernon smiles past everything — always has." Grandpa Dee was my dad's dad.

"What are you gonna do?" I said.

There was nothing she could do. It would just blow over. My dad wouldn't of left her, not in a million years.

He wanted attention from women, but he never would have left my mother.

"What can I do?" she said. "Maybe I should do some stepping-out myself, see how he likes it. Or go back to St. Joseph's, get started with nursing school."

"I thought you said your legs couldn't take it."

"I'm just getting too old, Elvis. I try to lose weight, but I gain ten pounds just walking past the icebox." She burst out laughing. "I'm so tired as it is — I don't got the energy to do no stepping-out. If I went out on a date, I'd probably fall asleep."

"You're beautiful, Momma."

"Oh, Elvis, I don't know what I'd do without you, honey. You're the light that gives me hope. Your life's gonna be different, you don't have to make the same mistakes as your daddy and me."

"Your life ain't over. You got a long time."

There were nine kids in Momma's family, the Smiths. The firstborn, Effie, died after a year. Then came Lillian, Levalle, and Rhetha, and two years later, my mother. The family half-starved most of the time, sharecroppers scratching out a living, always moving from place to place. That's where my mother's nerves came from. Everybody slept in one room, on crabgrass mattresses, in whatever shotgun shack or dilapidated house they found themselves in. Their Momma, my Grandma Doll, was an invalid, from TB, so things couldn't of been more precarious. They didn't even have money for shoes, the kids kept their soles together by putting hog rings around their toes. When they went to town they jingled like a band of gypsies. If it hadn't been for the generosity of neighbors, they'd a perished. All my mother's stuff with my dad, it was a replay of her childhood fears.

We heard my dad at the front porch. He had a hop in his step and a new gold shirt on. He was usually beat after work, but not this day; he was bright as the Fourth of July. My Daddy's life was a rollercoaster, up and down. He stood in front of Momma and me and glanced down at her slippers and housecoat. He didn't say anything, though. Momma looked away like he wasn't there. He said, "I got a job this evening. I'm gonna help Lamar deliver a horse over to Arkansas. We're gonna make forty bucks so I couldn't say no."

He waited for her to answer, but she just shrugged her shoulders and stared out the window. I hated this part. I wanted to walk out before things got started, but it's always hard to leave.

Finally Daddy said, "Now Gladys, don't be like this." My dad hated the silent treatment more than anything. I think he'd a preferred a frying pan over the head. "How can I turn down twenty bucks," he said, "that's nearly half-a-month's rent. Call Lamar if you don't believe me, he'll tell you. I'm just going over the bridge to Arkansas, it's not like I'm going off to war, Gladys."

"I'm defrosting a pork roast, Vernon. I was gonna fix us a nice supper." She knew what to say to make him feel guilty. "You can stay for supper," she said, "you and Lamar don't have to go traipsing over to Arkansas without dinner, do you?"

"We gotta get an early start so we can finish up before dark. It's four now, I gotta leave in an hour." The cuckoo clock went off. It was perfect, I felt like shooting us all, put us out of our misery.

My mother stood up and set herself. "You know I can't cook a pork roast in an hour, Vernon. It's not even thawed-out yet."

"Let's all sit down and eat something else," I said. Neither one of 'em answered me.

My dad was a sphinx, a mystery wrapped inside a riddle; nobody was gonna know his business if he could help it. He was secretive. I never knew half of what he did. The secrecy gave him a sense of power, though, and so did the lying. He always felt guilty anyway. I learned some of my bad tricks for him, that's for sure.

Momma sat back down on the sofa and stared at her woolly slippers. She said, "You go on with Lamar to that horse now."

"A man makes a few extra bucks, to make things easier for us, and this is all the thanks he gets. I'm gonna go wash up, Gladys."

We heard my dad draw a bath. Under her breath Momma said, "That horse they're delivering must be a filly."

Dixie

The months passed and I didn't hear from Sam Phillips. I was hoping to find a band to sing with, but nothing happened with that either. After Christmas I went into Sun to make another record. I didn't have anything to lose, but my lack of confidence showed. The new record wasn't as good as the first one. Sam Phillips said the same thing, he'd keep me in mind.

I went back to church, the Assembly of God Church on McLemore in South Memphis, and met Dixie Locke. I fell in love with her the first time I laid eyes on her. Dixie was all heart, I don't think she had a calculating bone in her body. At first I was too shy to talk to her, that's the way it was for me when I really liked somebody. One day after church, I overheard her tell a bunch of girlfriends, this was before we even met, that she was going roller-skating that Saturday night. At the time I wondered why she was talking so loud. Did she want me to overhear her? Turned out I was right.

I went out to the skating rink, the Rainbow Rollerdome on the outskirts of town on Lamar, hoping to run into her. I didn't know how to skate. This was my first time. It was a huge place, the size of an airplane hangar, there must of been a thousand people skating around the rink. I checked out skates from the rental shack, glad Dixie wasn't there yet.

I bounced my butt a half-a-dozen times on the hardwood straight-out, I was like a newborn foal finding my legs. A few years later I got into skating in a big way, started watching Roller Derby on TV and got addicted. Those girl skaters were bad, man, they were much rougher than the men. After I made it big, we rented the Rainbow for skating parties — we'd play Crack the Whip and War, full-body checks, the whole nine yards.

It was quite awhile before Dixie showed up. Then she came through the door with her friends, they were laughing and carrying-on. She was wearing a little black corduroy skirt and white tights. She had her own skates. It was the middle of winter and she didn't have a coat; I wondered if she'd half-froze to death coming over. She pretended like she didn't see me. That told me right there that she was interested. Two can play this game, I thought, I'll pretend I don't see her. I stood at the rail acting cool, trying to make sure my legs didn't cross so I wouldn't fall on my can. Dixie twirled around the rink a few times, her skirt flying out so I could see its white satin lining. She kept stealing glances my way.

After awhile she skated over to me. Good thing too, no way could I have skated over to her! She said, "I don't know if you remember me, but I've seen you at our church. My name's Dixie Locke."

"I know," I said. I sounded conceited but I was just scared. I liked her a lot and didn't know what to say, she was so beautiful. She reminded me of a Spanish dancer with her high forehead and brown, wide-set eyes.

"My name's Elvis Presley. Do you come here often?" I wanted to say something smart, but all I could think of was the oldest line in the world. Dixie's face was calm, confidence came natural for her.

"Yeah, about every weekend. A bunch of us come over." She pointed at her girlfriends. They were trying not to watch us and giggling amongst themselves. "We usually take the bus, unless we can get one of our moms to drive us over. I don't think I've seen you here before, Elvis."

"No, I can't say that you have. This is my first time." She swayed to the music and smiled at me.

"Then you don't know how to skate, huh?" She laughed and her dimples showed like a fairy from a storybook. She looked like a female Robin Hood, a forest of black hair with a knit cap on top. Skaters glided past us like a carousel; the marching music made it seem like we were all in a parade. Dixie's eyes kept changing colors like a kaleidoscope. I thought, my hunch was right, she's set it up for us to run into each other.

"I don't know how to skate, that's why my knuckles are turning white gripping this here rail. I'll have to learn, that is if I don't break my leg first. Say, would you like a Coke? We could go over to the snack bar and sit down."

"Sure, only maybe I'll have a Nehi." Dixie slipped her arm inside my elbow and we skated off the rink. I was afraid I'd fall, but my legs were steady. We took off our skates without saying a word. I was sure Dixie could see how alone I was. I wanted her to like me so bad.

We got our drinks and sat down at a table in the snack bar. "What high school you go to?" I said.

"Southside," she said. Dixie was younger than me, sixteen, but she was grown-up. She was the youngest of three, all girls, but the most levelheaded of the bunch. Dixie's parents looked to her to show her sisters the way.

"Do you like it?"

"It's all right. I'll be glad to get done, I got two more years. Seems like I been going to school forever." Dixie looked at me and thought about how different I was. She saw through me: I was lonely and needed somebody — the long hair and sideburns, the wild clothes — none of it made a bit of difference to her. She saw the person and didn't judge. It was Dixie's goodness I loved most.

"How 'bout you," she said. "Where'd you go to school? You're out, aren't you?"

"Yeah. I graduated last June, from Humes. I'm working now."

"Whereabouts?"

"At Precision Tool, over on Kansas. By you."

"You like it OK?"

"I make big bullets. 105 millimeter shells. Been doing it since I was fifteen. They used 'em over in Korea, and now the Army's stockpiling 'em. The work's all right, you gotta be fast and that makes the day go quick. I don't wanna stay there. I'll be finding something else pretty soon."

"I saw you singing with Cecil Blackwood and Jimmy Hamill after church last Sunday. You like to sing, Elvis?"

"Yeah, I do. I may try out for the Songfellows. I like singing gospel music." The Songfellows were a young gospel group the Blackwood Brothers sponsored at our church.

"You play, Elvis?"

"The guitar? Yeah, I do. I hunt and peck on the piano too, that's actually my favorite with the gospel. It feels like music's what I'm supposed to do." She pulled a napkin apart with her small hands and never took her eyes off me. I was telling her everything, she was easy to talk to.

"What do you mean, what you're supposed to do? You mean from God?'

"I guess so. I feel like He's got a plan for me, I think my calling's for the music. I know He wants me to help my parents."

"Why? What's wrong?"

"Nothing. They're OK. It's just they been working their whole lives and they're tired. I want to help them if I can." She thought about what I said. It was different for Dixie. Her daddy had always been the Rock of Gibraltar.

"Say, you wanna go back to town?" I said, "Maybe get a hamburger and milkshake at Leonard's or K's?"

"You got a car?"

"Yeah, a borrowed one," I said. I fibbed her about the borrowed car. I wanted to see if she'd go out with me if I didn't have a car.

"I gotta tell my friends, Elvis, and call my parents to see if it's OK."

"What you gonna tell 'em?"

"I'll say I wanna stay for the next skating session. It'll be OK." Right then I knew she was with me; not that I wanted her to start lying, but it showed she cared enough to take a risk for me.

Dixie went to the rail and waved her friends over. They giggled and skated over to us. She told them we were leaving together and I walked Dixie over to the telephone to call her momma. Little did I know she dialed an anonymous telephone number. She faked the call. She couldn't bear the thought of her mother saying no.

Driving back to town she sat close to me. It'd only been a few hours and we felt like a couple. Neither one of us could shut up. Dewey Phillips was on the radio. Dixie was a crazy fan of his too. I felt so cool driving into K's, everybody wondering who she was. We talked and ate hamburgers. She kissed me while we sat there, interrupted me right in the middle of a sentence with a peck on the lips. It was past midnight when I dropped her off at home. I was in love.

e   e   e

I always had a quick way of judging a show. If it made the world go away, like nothing else existed, or even mattered, then it was real gone. The Gospel Sings at Ellis Auditorium were those kind of shows. Four or five hours at a Sing and you not only forgot your problems, you were hard pressed to remember your name and address. They flat-out blew you away.

But gospel music was always my favorite. It's where I started and what I came back to. Growing up in Tupelo the whole family'd get together and sing: aunts, uncles, cousins, anybody who wanted to join in. We'd sit out on the front porch and sing spirituals, a little country too. My uncle Vester, and sometimes my grandpa J.D., would play the guitar. Somebody'd pick up a fiddle. These were the olden days before TV. Wasn't even much radio. Times were hard and people had to work day and night to put food on the table. All we had for hope was God and singing was our common prayer.

Dixie and me loved going to the Ellis Gospel Sings. Our love of God brought us together. Then success took us apart, no doubt about it. If I hadn't become a star I would have married Dixie. I'd be alive now, living in East Memphis, probably an electrician. Dixie and I would be spoiling the daylights out of our grandchildren. Dixie was my momma's favorite of all the girls I dated, they were good friends. She was the daughter my mother never had.

I remember our first Sing. It was a huge house at Ellis, even the galleries were packed. We got there early and heard the Speer Family and the Sunshine Boys, the Chuck Wagon Gang, then the Harmoneers. After the Harmoneers, the Statesmen were up with Jake Hess, my favorite singer. What a tenor voice the man had, the range and control, three octaves no problem, and phrasing, he was flawless. I'd played the Statesmen's records for Dixie at home, but this would be her first time to see them.

There was a drum roll and the crowd let out a roar as the Statesmen sprinted out on stage like a track club. For white guys they were pretty hip, especially for the times. This night they were wearing red double-breasted zoot suits with gold filigree thread, their hair stacked like sundaes in pomade and VO5 pompadours.

Dixie'd never seen anything like it. She squeezed my hand and put her arm around me and whispered in my ear above the noise of the crowd. "Where'd they get those suits, Elvis? And the hair, I gotta find out who their hairdresser is. You all must shop at the same store, Lansky's, right?" She tried to tickle me in the ribs but I bounced away.

"Yeah, I've seen them in Lansky's," I laughed. I hugged her tight and kissed her. I was so happy I'd found somebody who understood me and my crazy ways. "Only when they go in," I said, "they can buy whatever they want."

"One of these days you will too, Elvis."

The Statesmen opened with "Peace in the Valley," breaking the quartet up into duets. The start of an act is like a jumbo jet revving for take-off. A crowd's energy corkscrews higher and higher; it's like a flame if you have the eyes to see it. I almost did when I was alive. It was just beyond the veil.

Hovie Lister, the great piano player and leader of the Statesmen, was off to the side, deadpan like always. That was Hovie's schtick, no matter what kind of mayhem the Statesmen put a crowd to. Jake Hess and Jim Wetherington took turns taking solos. People began to swoon in the aisles, hollering-out "Hallelujah." It blew Dixie's mind. I was used to it from the revivals in Tupelo growing up.

I leaned over to Dixie and whispered, "They're just getting warmed up, wait till they get going." I really wanted Dixie to like the Statesmen too. I needed the person I was with to share my passions. Jake Hess finished up "Peace in the Valley" with a soprano flourish. His vibrato was beyond compare, the man could've sung opera. The crowd was fusing into one pulsing mass. It's like a beating heart when a crowd becomes one.

"He's even better than on the records, Elvis." She was talking about Jake Hess. "I see what you mean now about voice control. Jake can do anything, it's amazing."

They did "I Believe in the Man in the Sky" next. Rocked it pretty good, too. Hovie Lister barrelhoused the rhythm line and Big Chief Jim Wetherington, the Statesmen's bass singer, started shaking it up. I'll tell you, Chief had more moves than Bekins. Man was a dervish, make his legs and hips go in different directions like a slinky toy. Wanna know who I learned from, look no further than Jim.

Lot of people think gospel music is slow and subdued, something only for church, but it's got a bigger beat than the blues. Once you get the beat you can take it any which way, move from lead to rhythm and back again. It's call and response, just like the blacks singing in the cotton fields. Gospel is where rhythm and blues comes from. The Statesmen were doing the same stuff black rhythm 'n' blues guys had been doing for years.

The crowd, particularly the women, were going nuts over the Chief. Dixie let out a shout, then looked over at me to see if it was OK. It was OK with me, I was taking notes! "Does the Chief always do this?" Dixie asked, and she did a shimmy like Mata Hari and fluttered her eyes. She laughed and threw her arms around me and whispered in my ear, "You can move like that, I've seen you."

"Maybe I ought to sing that way too," I said, winking at her.

"I don't know about that, Elvis, then I'd be sharing you with all these screaming females." She looked around at the commotion Chief was causing and said, "Yeah! I think you should." I spun her around like a top and she nearly fell down laughing. I loved Dixie's spirit.

Next the Statesmen did their hit, "Jesus Walked that Lonesome Valley," in one, long rolling encore that lasted for twenty minutes. People were jumping up and down and singing hallelujah. It was God-intoxication. All a performer does is strike the match — joy's just waiting to come out of folks.

The Statesmen were done for awhile, but they'd be back. The All Night Sings gave you course after course. I asked Dixie if she wanted to meet the Statesmen. I used to go backstage sometimes at the Sings and meet the singers; they all knew I was into gospel music and wanted to be a singer. That's how I met Jake Hess, and J.D. Sumner too.

"Do you think we could, Elvis, I mean they wouldn't mind?" Dixie asked.

I played it cool like I was big man on campus. "Naw, they won't mind," I said, "We should wait till the show's over though, then everybody'll just be relaxing." I wanted to impress her, why I don't know, she was already with me a thousand percent. "I'll introduce you to the Chief, and Jake, J.D. Sumner, you already know James Blackwood."

"I don't know, Elvis," she said, "you're the musician, what would I say to them?" She was feeling embarrassed like she wasn't good enough. I see now it was my ego-trip that intimidated her. I'd get pumped up like this and show off and name-drop, and then the people around me would feel like they didn't count.

The Blackwood Brothers were up next. They were members of our Assembly of God congregation, so Dixie and me knew them. Precision, that was the Blackwood's genius, their harmonies were polished as a cloud. They were the Bachs of gospel music. They were all fine gentlemen too. It was my pleasure over the years to be their friend. The Blackwoods were my momma's favorite. (They sang at her funeral.) On this particular night they wore dark suits and white shirts, thin blue ties, hair slicked back real clean. They started off with "Rock of Ages."

With the Statesmen it was one crescendo after another until you were wrung out like a dishrag, but the Blackwood's music was a journey of the soul. It was the simplicity and purity of their harmony, the layerings of sound. In a medley, they went on to "Amazing Grace." Everybody stood, listening with their hearts. You can see it on peoples' faces — their mouths drop open a little — a crowd becomes a sea of glistening eyes. I looked over at Dixie and saw tears on her face. I was crying too.

I closed my eyes and squeezed Dixie's hand as they sang "How Great Thou Art," my favorite gospel song. She crossed her fingers into mine. I felt our lives, our light, pass into one another.

It was late and I didn't want Dixie's parents to worry about her. We'd left the car at Alabama Street and walked over, so we walked back home. We walked slowly, under a canopy of stars, our arms around each other. It was springtime and already warm.

"It was wonderful, Elvis. Thank you so much." Dixie's face was fresh as a flower. I couldn't believe how much I loved her. My heart felt so much peace. Dixie said, "The whole world looks sparkly, doesn't it, Elvis, the cars and the streets, it's all sparkling in Jesus. Look at the moon." Dixie pointed to the sky. "It's a crescent with one big star." Her smile was broad as the Milky Way.

I said, "I always feel brand new after a Sing, cleansed in spirit." And I did, I felt light as a feather.

Dixie squeezed me and put her arms around my neck. She said, "I love you, Elvis."

I told her I loved her too. We stopped and kissed underneath the light at the entrance of St. Mary's Church, across the street from the Courts. It was same corner Billie Wardlaw and me had broke up at a few years before, but now I was with the woman I wanted to marry.

"You could do it, Elvis," she said, "be a gospel singer. Your voice is beautiful. You got the feeling, too, darling." It was bright as day underneath the church light. "I think you should do it," she said.

Job Had It Harder

The next day, Sunday, I had an audition with the Songfellows, the youth gospel group the Blackwood Brothers sponsored at our church. It was a spur-of-the-moment thing; after Bible study Jimmy Hamill, one of the members of the group, asked me if I wanted to try out. He said one of the fellas in the group might leave soon and they needed to have somebody lined up. It was kinda silly for them to audition me really, we sang together all the time — they knew what I could do.

We went to one of the rooms at the back of the church off the dining room. It was just Cecil Blackwood, Jimmy, and myself. I knew Cecil from the Courts, he'd moved in there with his new wife just as my folks and me were moving out. Cecil's uncle, James Blackwood, was one of the original members of the Blackwood Brothers, and Jimmy's dad was the pastor of the church, Reverend

James Hamill. We'd all gotten to know each other through Christ Ambassadors, the young men's Christian group at the church.

It was funny with auditions, I always knew beforehand how they'd go. I didn't have a good feeling about this one walking through the door. Jimmy Hamill asked me what I wanted to sing. I said, "Let's try 'Peace in the Valley.'" I figured we all knew it and I could go with the lead or rhythm. Before we started, Jimmy said, "Hey Cecil, you think Elvis'll be up to singing today? He's not wearing his lightning bolts." Jimmy was talking about the pair of trousers I had with the pink stripes down the sides. "The boy may not have the power without those pants," Jimmy said, "or maybe Elvis is like Samson and the power's in his long hair."

I smiled and said, "Well, I'll just have to make do," but inside my stomach tightened-up like a vise. I didn't know where I stood with these guys. We were friends in the youth group, and we sang together a lot, but there was always the little digs about me being strange.

I started up on "Peace in the Valley," we were just playing guitars. *"I'm tired and so weary but I must go alone ... if the Lord comes and calls me, calls me away."* I felt a sense of peace as soon as I started singing. That's why I liked gospel music so much, it brought me to peace the same as prayer. *"... Well, the mornings so light ... and the night is black as the sea."* Their voices fell in behind me as we went to the refrain, *"There will be*

peace in the valley for me someday, oh Lord I pray ...
There will be no sadness, no sorrow, no trouble, no
trouble I see ... ." I forgot about Jimmy's digs, I took my
voice down and sang bass; Jimmy smiled at me and took
over the lead. Both Jimmy and Cecil were fine singers
and musicians, they went on to have big careers in
gospel, Cecil with the Blackwood Brothers and Jimmy
with the Kingsmen.

We got done with "Peace in the Valley" and I felt good.
They were gonna decide whatever they wanted with the
audition, didn't make any difference what I thought
about it. Cecil started up on "Down by the Riverside,"
which was always one of my favorites. We sung it in
rounds, each taking a part and syncopating the beat. I
picked up a pair of drumsticks from the top of the piano
and rattled out a rhythm line behind Jimmy's guitar. *"I'm*
gonna lay down my burden, down by the riverside ... I
ain't gonna study war no more, ain't gonna study war
no more ... I'm gonna lay down my sword and shield,
down by the riverside." We rocked the song pretty good
and were having a great time.

We kept on with the high-spirited spirituals, "Joshua
Fit the Battle" and "When the Saints Go Marchin' In."
Since it was an audition, I wondered why we weren't
doing any slow numbers, but it was their call. I'd forgotten all about the lead weight in my stomach, so I was
brought up short by what Jimmy said when we finished.

He looked me straight in the face and said, "Elvis, why

don't you give it up? You can't sing. You will never be a singer." I felt like he'd hit me between the eyes with a railroad car. Cecil Blackwood looked away. He saw how hurt I was, but he didn't say anything. I was speechless.

I picked up my stuff and got set to go. As I was walking out Jimmy said, "You sang alright, Elvis, don't worry about it. I don't think there's a place opening up in the group anyhow. We'll talk more about it if it does. Don't take what I said bad, Elvis."

I drove home in a daze. I was angry but didn't know it, not right away — I felt stupid, like I'd been discovered for how meager and unworthy I was. All the cars and people on the street looked far away like they were in a silent movie.

I drove straight home to Alabama Street, hoping my mother would be there. She wasn't, she'd gone somewhere with my dad. The house felt unnatural, scary. I went into my room and flopped down on the bed. My eyes burned and I fought back tears. I tried to understand how Jimmy could've said what he did. He doesn't mean to be mean, I thought, he's just full of himself — maybe he's jealous of me. I stared at the cracks in the ceiling, and slowly, I came back to my flesh. I heard the blood rushing through my ears, and I fell asleep.

I woke up when my parents came home. I wanted to talk to my momma but I didn't wanna tell my dad what happened. She hollered in to me, "You home, Elvis?" I pretended to be asleep. She peeked in and told my dad I was taking a nap. I knew Daddy would leave soon. I heard him tell Momma he was going out to work on the car and that I should come out and help him when I woke up. The door slammed, I felt heavy as a sack of rice — but I dragged myself into the kitchen.

I told her everything and she listened like always. She knew to just lemme talk when something was really bothering me. I talked for long time, watching Daddy out the window wax the car.

I wanted to tell Dixie right away. I even drove over to her house that evening to talk about it, but the light in her bedroom was off and I didn't go in. I sorted things out myself, and then I didn't feel like telling her. I was afraid Dixie'd see me as a loser. She wouldn't of, of course, as I later found out when I told her, but that was my fear and shame.

I got real negative and down on myself, thought I should give up my dream and go for something realistic like a trade or driving truck. All of it made me depressed, though; that's what happens when you give up what you most want.

That next Sunday I didn't even go to church. I called Dixie and said I had too many chores to do at home. "Are you all right?" she asked. "I'm fine," I said.

I went on like this for a couple of weeks, down in the dumps, telling myself it was OK if I didn't make it with the music. Then one night before bed, it was a Friday night, I was saying my prayers and I heard a voice inside me. At first I thought it was just my own thoughts, then I realized it was somebody else's voice. It was Jessie. "Is that you?" I said.

"Yes, it's me." He said. I'd almost forgotten about talking to him as a boy.

"Don't worry," he said, "everything's gonna work out fine. There's a plan for you, Elvis. You know that."

"I hope so," I said, "I'm feeling pretty low."

"Faith isn't given, you have earn it, Elvis."

"I don't understand," I said.

"It's a challenge, a test, when you feel like this. It's not supposed to be easy."

"What? This all's a test from God?"

"No. Not from God. This all's a test from you. But that's not important now. What is important is your faith. Do you know why you forgot about me?"

"I don't know," I said.

"Because you stopped believing I'm here. You're making things harder than they are. Do you know why?"

"No."

"You wanna be right and figure everything out. You feel like you gotta be in charge, that's why you keep worrying how things are gonna turn out."

"I don't wanna fail. Daddy says ... he's never seen a guitar player who was worth a damn. I get so discouraged."

"It's not supposed to be easy, Elvis."

"We'all suppose to be like Job, huh?"

"Job had it harder than you, Elvis."

"That's true." I laughed. "Jessie, there's something else."

"What is it?"

"It's Momma and Daddy. I'm worried about 'em. Do you know what I mean?"

"Yes."

"What can I do? Both of 'em are to blame, they're like little kids."

"They have to solve their own problems, that's how it is. You're gonna be able to help them like you want, Elvis."

"Buy them a house?"

"Yes. A lot more too."

"With the music? Am I just making this all up? Are you really here, Jessie?"

"Yes. I am."

"Where are you? Are you here or in heaven?"

"I'm here, and I'm there at the same time."

"You always been here, always been with me?"

"Yes."

"There's something else, Elvis, I have some things to say about your music too."

"What?"

"You know how to do it already. The music. Just let it happen."

Hi Hat

After the Songfellows blackballed me, I decided it was time to get out of Precision Tool. I just figured it made sense to cover all my bases, learn a trade while I pursued the music. I wasn't that discouraged with music — Jessie had helped with that — it was just time to move on. I heard about a job opening up at Crown Electric from a couple of my music friends, Johnny and Dorsey Burnette.

Crown was right around the corner from our house, on Poplar. I drove a truck to start with, delivered wire and supplies to job sites, but there was the chance to apprentice as an electrician and get started with night classes. The Tiplers, Jim and Gladys, the owners of Crown Electric, were great. They could see I was willing to work hard and get ahead. It was forty bucks a week to start, which was less than Precision Tool, but at least there was a future to it.

A few weeks after I started at Crown, I got another tryout for a band. I ran into a friend of mine, Ronnie Smith, at Cotton Carnival and he said I ought to audition for the Stompers, a band he was in with Eddie Bond. Ronnie said he'd set it up for the next day, a Saturday night. That day I went over to Dixie's early to tell her the good news.

Only Mr. Locke was there, Dixie and Mrs. Locke had gone out shopping. Mr. Locke was the strong, silent type, six-foot-two and two-forty with arms the size of watermelons. He was in his chair reading the paper when I came up the steps and he waved to me through the screen door to come on in. "Good afternoon, Mr. Locke," I said, "You all gone to Cotton Carnival the last couple of days?" Cotton Carnival was Memphis's cotton jubilee held the middle of May every year.

"We went downtown to Court Square, they were fixing to pick the Cotton Queen," Mr. Locke said, "Too many people for me though, it gets bigger every year. Elvis, you done cut your hair, what's got into you? You musta lost a bet, son."

"Naw, I get haircuts, Mr. Locke, you all just don't notice. I got a band tryout tonight, so I thought it'd be good to get it cut."

"Why sure, this way you're presentable." He was starting to cotton to me.

Through the window I saw Dixie's mother pull in the driveway. "Say, Mr. Locke," I said, "could you do me a favor and not say anything about the band tryout? I wanna tell Dixie myself."

Dixie came through the door with her arms full of groceries. "Elvis, you got here early," she said, "I didn't think you'd come by till five."

I took the groceries from her. "I'm not too early am I?" I hadn't seen her in a few days, and man, she looked good!

"No, of course not, honey. I'll get ready and we can go downtown." I loved the sound of her voice, it was like a song.

"There ain't no rush," I said, "let's go sit out on the porch, I got something to tell you."

"What is it?"

"You help your momma put the groceries away, then I'll tell you." Dixie looked at her parents and shrugged her shoulders. I went out on the front porch and sat down on the swing. All the neighborhood kids were out in the street playing bikes and jumping rope. It was a cute little house they had, nothing fancy. Dixie and her sisters all slept in the same room. The lawn was perfect and Mrs. Locke had planted flowers everywhere. It was the first hot night of summer and it was great to smell honeysuckle, and roses, again. It felt like weeks since I'd taken a deep breath and relaxed.

Inside I heard Mrs. Locke question Dixie about what she was wearing. "You're not gonna wear those Capri pants downtown on a Saturday night, Dixie, that blouse is too tight." I glanced down at my bolero jacket and hot-pink, ruffled shirt. I bet Mrs. Locke thinks it's me corrupting Dixie, I thought. Inside, Dixie was saying, "Oh Momma, this is what all the girls wear. You're not happy unless I'm wearing a dress."

Dixie came out and sat beside me. "Now what's this news of yours?"

"I ran into Ronnie Smith last night at Cotton Carnival and he said the Stompers, you know with Eddie Bond, are looking for a singer. They're getting lots of gigs, even working some weeknights." I'd played some gigs with Ronnie around town, lodge dances and stuff like that. Dixie was friends with Ronnie too, they both went to Southside High.

"That's wonderful, Elvis, see I told you something good was gonna work out for you," Dixie said. "I thought it'd be gospel, with a quartet, but this sounds good too." She put her hands in mine, her eyes were bright. "All you need is a start, darling, and then you'll be on your way. You'll see."

I hadn't told her about the Songfellows rejecting me. My pride was holding me back. I didn't see that Dixie loved me, all I could think about was measuring-up. I sat quiet for a moment.

"There's something I need to tell you, Dixie."

"What?"

"I had my tryout with the Songfellows, with Cecil and Jimmy. They blackballed me."

"No. That couldn't be," she said. I saw deep hurt in her eyes. "You're not kidding me, Elvis, are you?"

"No. I done tried out but didn't make it."

"What happened? What were they thinking about?" Her voice rose in anger. It felt good to have her care so much. "Look how folks gather 'round at McKellar Lake to hear you play. I'm gonna talk to 'em. They done made a mistake."

"It doesn't matter, probably wouldn't of worked out anyhow." Dixie saw my weakness and it only made her love me more.

"I won't go talk to 'em, Elvis, don't worry. I'm not gonna embarrass you." Her face was burning. "I just feel so bad for you, honey. You got just as good a voice as any of them ... better!"

"It takes a while to get a break," I said, "but you only need one."

"You got more talent than all of them, Elvis. I gotta ask you something."

"What is it?"

"Don't take this wrong, now, but are you going after Ronnie and the Stompers cause of what happened at church? I'm worried that you're giving up on gospel music cause of those brats. There's a lot of other gospel groups, Elvis, you don't have to pay them any mind."

I was set to say no, but then I thought, maybe she's right, I have written off gospel music. I said, "Something'll work out, I just can't get discouraged."

Dixie said, "Don't let anything stop you, Elvis." She was young and beautiful but there was steel in her. "When is this tryout of yours with Eddie Bond and the Stompers, Elvis?"

I said, "Well ... it's right now! I'm suppose to be over at the Hi Hat at eight."

"The club over on Third?" Dixie said.

"Yeah, that's the place. They're gonna have me sing a few songs before they go on."

"Do you want me to come along?" Dixie asked. She looked like a kid afraid of missing Christmas.

"Course I want you there. Somebody's gotta clap for me. You will, won't you?"

"Silly," she shouted, "of course I will." We kissed, not caring if Mr. and Mrs. Locke were looking.

e   *e*   *e*

We drove over to the Hi Hat on South Third, it was right around the corner from Dixie's house. It was a typical run-down beer joint, had a neon sign out front with a top hat and cane. I wanted to sing with a band so bad. My insides churned. I thought, at least Dixie's with me and I don't have to be alone.

Dixie was uptight too. She was afraid somebody from Railway Express, where her dad worked, would see her in a honky-tonk. We didn't even know if she could get in, being sixteen. We walked from the sun into the darkness of the Hi Hat, the bartender looked us over, a cigarette between his lips, and said, "Pardon me, but how old are you two?" I told him I'd come to sing with the band, asked him if Dixie and me could drink Cokes. He glanced at Dixie, who looked a couple years older than she was, and said, "OK, why don't you all sit on the other side of the dance floor over there, away from the bar."

He poured our Cokes. The Hi Hat was your average dive, dark and dingy and smelling of beer. The place was empty except for a few guys joking quietly at the bar while they watched a prize fight on TV. I didn't see the band anywhere, but we were early. It was a pretty good-sized place with a stage and space for people to dance. We sat down at a table against the far wall, underneath a neon Hamm's Beer sign with those silly bears.

Eddie Bond walked through the back door of the club with a couple members of the group. They were carrying their instruments. Ronnie hadn't arrived yet so I wondered if I should introduce myself. Didn't have to though, Eddie Bond laid his guitar down on the stage and came over to us.

"Hi, I'm Eddie Bond, Elvis." He smiled and nodded Dixie's way. Eddie was a real brash kid and a pretty fair musician; he wrote "The Ballad of Buford Pusser," which became the movie *Walking Tall*.

"Pleasure to meet you," I said, "this is Dixie Locke, my girlfriend."

"Pleasure to make your acquaintance, Dixie," he smiled at her, "Elvis is a lucky man." That put me off, I was sensitive to even the insinuation that somebody was after the girl I was with. Dixie didn't have any reaction so I settled down. "Elvis, what do you say you sing a few songs before we get started. Let's see what you got."

I said, "OK," and looked around to see if Ronnie Smith had shown up. He had. He was standing at the bar with the other members of the band watching us. Dixie and me waved, and Ronnie waved back.

I grabbed my guitar and went up on stage. There was only about twenty people there, including the band. I started off with Hank Williams' song, "Lovesick Blues." I thought it'd be perfect for the Hi Hat. There was only one spotlight, and it was shining right in my eyes; I couldn't see the audience at all. The song came out good, though, I thought I captured its feeling of loneliness. There was polite applause, except for Dixie of course, she clapped like crazy.

I went on to "Til I Waltz Again With You," the song I did at the Humes Minstrel Show. I had the song down cold, it came out even better than "Lovesick Blues." I got a good round of applause and was pretty pleased with myself. Eddie Bond gave me an OK sign and waved me over. I wanted to do more, but the two songs were enough. I took off my guitar and looked at Dixie. She blew me a kiss.

I thought Eddie'd be pleased with the audition. I got over to him and he reached out and put his arm around my shoulder. Ronnie and the other members of the group stepped away knowing our conversation was private. Eddie drew me close like a buddy and said, "It was pretty good, Elvis," he paused and looked me in the eye, "but I don't think you're ever gonna make it as a singer. If I was you, I'd stick to driving truck."

I went dark inside and all I wanted was to get his arm off me. "OK Eddie," I said. "I understand."

My heart was broken, and believe me, I didn't understand at all.

e   *e*   *e*

I couldn't tell Dixie what Eddie Bond had said. I was just too embarrassed. I went back to our table and said, "Let's go." Dixie looked bewildered, as if to say, that's all, two songs and we're outta here? I shut Dixie out, but when I hurt this bad the only person I could talk to was my momma.

We went over to Rocky's at McKellar Lake and listened to music. I wanted to forget I'd ever laid eyes on Eddie Bond. I was good at hiding my feelings, Dixie couldn't tell how bad I felt. "You all right, Elvis?" she asked.

"Yeah, I'm fine," I said.

I went home and tried to get some sleep. My head felt like it was full of bees. Later, I woke up in the middle of the night and my mind was clear. Inside my heart I called out to Jessie, "What am I suppose to do?"

"You're not supposed to be singing with the Stompers," he said.

"What should I do then? I'm so tired of failing."

"It's gonna happen for you, Elvis. I told you, faith's not supposed to be easy. Feel what you feel, deep down."

"I can play a little, but not enough to be a professional."

"What do you feel, Elvis?"

"I guess I feel like I failed."

"You haven't failed; you haven't even got started yet. But what else?"

"I don't know."

"Fear," Jessie said, "You're afraid."

"I guess I am, maybe that is what I feel."

"You think just cause Eddie Bond doesn't want you that you failed."

"Yeah."

"You're not supposed to be singing with Eddie Bond."

"What then?"

"Pay attention to what you feel inside when you sing. Go deep."

"What do you mean?"

"Just feel it in your body and let the songs take their shape. The rest will happen from that."

Fate

At the end of June, Marion Keisker called and wanted to know if I could come over, right then, and sing a few songs for Sam Phillips. I was over there before she put the receiver down. It'd only taken Sam Phillips a year to give me a call back! I guess that qualifies as an overnight sensation. The Bible says, "Blessed are those who wait on the Lord." And it's true, the path of faith requires our patience, and holding good thoughts too. A good thought draws fate like a magnet.

I got to Sun and Marion was excited. "Sam has a song for you to do. Isn't it wonderful? I know you're gonna do great, Elvis, I know it." Sam heard me come in and walked into the foyer. He was wearing a pair of pastel green slacks and a white polo shirt. He was smiling and whistling and in an upbeat mood. We shook hands and he said, "I'm glad you had time to come over, Elvis." Time to come over? I thought. I'll move a cot in if that's what you want. I looked down and saw I hadn't changed my pants. I was wearing my black pegged slacks with the electric-pink lightning bolts. But it didn't make a bit of difference to him.

He wanted to make conversation. "What have you been up to, son?" he said. His eyes were calm and that relaxed me a little.

"I got a new job. I'm not at Precision Tool anymore. I'm over at Crown Electric, learning to be an electrician. I'm driving a truck now but there's a chance to move up. I'm taking classes."

"Do you know Johnny Burnette? He's over at Crown too. Or he was. Johnny's recorded for me." I peeked past him into the recording studio. It all looked the same.

"Sure, I know Johnny, and Dorsey, his brother. They're from my neighborhood. He's not at Crown anymore, though. I got his job, I think."

"Well, that's good. For both of you. I guess Johnny's doing music full-time. I got a song here that I think you can sing. I think your voice is right for it."

"I'll give it a try. Yes, sir. What's it called?"

"It's called 'Without You.' I thought about you singing it the first time I heard it." I was surprised he'd thought about me at all. "Let's go on back into the studio and you can take a look at it, Elvis."

I'll tell you, it was a weird song, kind of pub crying music, sounded like Irish blues. But I was happy just to be in Sun Studios doing an audition. I would of sung anything.

By the time we got done with the song, I thought the title, "Without You," referred to yours truly. Lots of times I could pick up something pretty quick. Not this day. I was too uptight. I told him straight out, "I can't sing it." I know he respected me for that.

"You gotta get used to recording," he said. "It's like riding a bike, at first it's tough and then it comes natural. I want you to sing some more songs for me. Anything you really feel down deep. Just pretend like you're not even here, like you're playing in your own room." Fat chance, I thought, I know exactly where I am — in Sun Studios auditioning for Sam Phillips!

"OK," I said. "How 'bout 'Til I Waltz Again With You,' the Teresa Brewer song?" It was the first tune that popped into my head. I sang it and just about everything else I knew too. I did some Eddy Arnold and Hank Williams, Dean Martin's "That's Amore" and the Ames Brothers' "Rag Mop." Some Bing Crosby, "Harbor Lights," and some spirituals, "How Great Thou Art" and "I Believe in the Man in the Sky." I went through everything I knew and was down to snatches of this and that.

He kept saying, "You're trying too hard, Elvis, just relax and let it come. Don't try to sing like anybody." It was just him and me, all afternoon. I sweated through my clothes while Sam looked cool as a daisy. He wasn't worried a bit about wasting time, he was relaxed and enjoyed it. Sam knew it was gonna take me time. I was tuckered out, but I didn't feel it until we were nearly done.

Finally Sam said, "Let's call it a day, Elvis. You've done good. I'm not sure what we got. I'll listen to the tapes. You got an interesting voice, son. I don't know what we can do with it. But we'll see."

I was silent for a minute cause I didn't know what he intended. "I sure appreciate the chance to come over and do this for you, Mr. Phillips." I was worried he wouldn't want me back. Then I thought, he's the one who called me, and he isn't saying no.

I said, "I can learn anything you want." I couldn't hide how much I needed him to want me. He saw. Mr. Sam imagined himself in my shoes and didn't hold it against me. The man had compassion.

"That's probably how it'll go," he said. "It takes a little time. You got to work at it. I'll think about who you might get with. I have some guys in mind. You get with them and practice some songs. See what you all come up with. I'll call you about it."

Driving home I had to pinch myself, I'd spent the afternoon with Sam Phillips making a record. And this time I hadn't paid for it! Nobody was home so I called Dixie.

"Guess what I did this afternoon?" I said.

"Lemme guess, you put new brakes on your car?"

"Nope. It was music."

"I don't know, silly," she said. "What did you do?"

"Had an audition with Mr. Sam Phillips of Sun Records."

"The guy you've been hoping would call? Oh my goodness, what'd he say?" I didn't know what to tell her, so much had happened.

"He's gonna listen to the tapes. He wants me to sing with some guys."

e   *e*   *e*

A few days later the Blackwood Brothers' plane crashed at Clanton, Alabama. It was a Wednesday night, June 30, 1954. They'd been at the Chilton County Peach Festival at the Fairgrounds in Clanton. They had a noon show with the Statesmen and Jake Hess. Afterwards, they stayed on for the afternoon's festivities. When it got time for 'em to leave, R.W. Blackwood and Bill Lyles, another member of the group, tried a take off from the Fairgrounds to check out the clearance.

They took off OK, but when they went to land R.W. did a power dive. Everybody thought he was showing off, but they didn't pull out.

They crashed and burned with everybody watching. James Blackwood ran for the plane saying he was going in to rescue them. Jake Hess had to put a bear hug on him, otherwise he'd a died too. It was chaos. No one could believe it.

Driving home that night to Memphis, James Blackwood swore he'd never sing again. Jake Hess told him he owed it to people to go on.

The next morning Crown Electric was quiet as a tomb. Jim Tipler, the owner of Crown, took me aside and told me what happened. I kept hoping it was a dream as I loaded up the paneled truck. It was a hot morning, unnatural, must of been 100 degrees at seven-thirty in the morning. Felt like all the life been sucked out of the air. I saw people driving down Poplar holding their hands to their faces and sobbing. I reckoned they'd just heard about R.W. and Bill. I imagined them on stage, full of life, and it made me wild with pain.

In the truck I could cry. I listened to reports all day on the radio, switching from station to station to get the latest news. The town was stunned. The Blackwoods were our stars, and now this. All I wanted was to get off work and see Dixie. I could've called her, but I wanted to see her. The hours passed slow.

When I got to Dixie's she was crying. The Blackwoods were the backbone of our church. Ruth Lyles, Bill's wife, was Dixie's Sunday school teacher. They were close. Losing R.W. and Bill was losing members of our family.

Dixie hugged me and said, "How can it be, Elvis, they're so young and with little kids. How could God take them?" There was such confusion and fear in her eyes. I held her tight; I wanted to lose myself inside her. I didn't wanna break down in front of Mr. and Mrs. Locke so we took off to Gaston Park. The sun was still high up in the sky and cruel as the devil.

We found a park bench and held hands, staring off into space. All the life had been drained from us. We sat a long time without saying a thing — grief's like walking a desert — finally Dixie said, "I don't how they're gonna go on. And the kids, what must they feel, Elvis? I don't know what I'd do if my daddy died." She started sobbing really hard. I put my arms around her and my tears came. We cried so much that our clothes got wet. I'd never felt so close to her.

Dixie said, "Do you think they'll keep going, Elvis? Is this the end of the quartet? How can they do it without R.W. and Bill?" She reminded me of my mother. They both felt pain so deep.

I said, "They got to, Dixie. God wouldn't want them to stop."

I took off my shoes and felt the grass under my feet. There was bushes in bloom across the way. I went over to pick the yellow flowers for Dixie. I thought about Jessie. I can talk to him and he's dead.

Dixie came over and tapped me on the shoulder. "I thought about you all day, driving the truck; I couldn't wait for you to get off work and come over." I kissed her. It was different from any time before. For her too. We needed each other so bad; there was nothing for either one of us to hang on to except each other. All the loss and sorrow and confusion of the moment, gave wings to our kisses, returning our flesh to Spirit.

I said, "What do you think death is, Dixie? I don't think people are just dead and gone." For a second I saw myself in a river standing on cobblestones. It was the flow of Soul and Spirit moving through me.

Dixie said, "The funeral's tomorrow. Governor Clement's coming over. I wanna go together, Elvis." Dixie was going on vacation to Florida with her family in a couple of days and it'd be the first time we'd been apart. I didn't want her to ever leave me; but I didn't wanna say so and make her feel bad.

The sprinklers came on and the blackbirds took after the worms. We stood in the rainbows, our arms around each other's waist. I thought about being a bird and not having to know of death.

Dixie said, "I never want you to die, Elvis. Promise me you won't." The sun was bright-white on her face.

"I promise," I said.

Dixie smiled and said, "It feels like we're married, darling."

"It does," I said, and I heard the most beautiful music inside me.

e   e   e

I felt like a leaf on the wind. Death was ticking inside me and I wanted to run. I was curious too, though. I thought death would take me to God. Didn't make the pain any easier, though. I dreaded the memorial service. I didn't know if I had another tear left in me. It was the biggest crowd I'd ever seen at Ellis Auditorium. They had to open up the North Hall after the South filled; the galleries were packed with black folks. The Blackwoods were beloved and the whole community turned out. It was the biggest funeral in the history of Memphis.

Dixie and I sat middle front with Momma and Daddy. Jake Hess sang "How Great Thou Art" and the Speer Family sang too. What a mixture of joy and sadness, there wasn't a dry eye in the house. Governor Clement gave the best speech I'd ever heard. He talked about what R.W. and Bill had stood for — integrity in the grace of God — and how their love could never die or be undone. Pastor Hamill from our church talked about Bill and R.W. as men and deacons of the congregation. He said it was not ours to know the mind of God.

My mother hadn't cried like this since Aunt Rhetha died.

After the service, I went over to Dixie's and spent the evening. I didn't have much to say. I shuffled my feet and stared at the carpet. Later we went outside on the swing and held each other. It was after midnight when I got home.

I fell fast asleep and had a dream. I was with my dad in downtown Memphis and we'd just moved from Tupelo. I was thirteen. We were walking down Adams and there in front of us was the Shelby County Courthouse in the sunset. It looked like from ancient Greek times. My dad put his arm around me and we walked over to its steps.

He talked on about how good Memphis was while I stood awestruck at the grandeur of the courthouse. It looked like the capitol of the universe with its columns stretching to infinity. I left my dad and walked up the steps. Inside was a park filled with people from foreign countries, and off on a hillside was a graveyard.

I walked to the graves with the sunset in front of me burning red and pale green. The gravestones set in a carpet of deep green lawn. Aunt Rhetha was there, and Jessie. And Mississippi Slim, the cowboy singer who got me started back in Tupelo. I wondered if he was dead.

I looked out on the park below. There were people from all over the world, Eskimos carrying harpoons and East Indians with jewels between their eyes, white people with piercing eyes and strong jaws, and African dancers and drummers. They were carrying books and papers to show each other. It was a university of learning and each of them was a piece of the puzzle.

Then I woke up. The dream had been so real I felt like a stranger in my own bed. "Jessie, what was that, what does it mean?" I was half asleep and spoke right out loud.

"It's where you're going, Elvis."

I thought he was saying I was dying. "You mean to death?"

"No. Not that. You're going to learning."

It's Alright

Scotty Moore, who was to become my lead guitarist, called while I was at the movies. My mother answered the phone. He introduced himself and said he represented Sun Records. She knew the call was important. This was a week after my audition with Sam Phillips, though I'd lost track of time after the Blackwoods' plane crash. "I'll go get him at the movie," she told Scotty, but he said just to wait till I got in.

She headed straight over to the Suzores. I saw her standing in the aisle looking for me with a piece of paper in her hand. "Sun Records called, Elvis." She read Scotty's name from the light of the movie screen. "Come on home and call him, honey."

Soon as we got through the door I picked up the phone. Scotty's wife, Bobbie, answered and in a minute Scotty came on. "Hope I didn't drag you outta the movies, Elvis. This can wait you know, I told your momma that." I liked Scotty right away. He didn't have an ounce of bs in him.

"Naw," I said. "The movie was over."

"Sam Phillips thought it'd be good idea to have you come by and play with us, sing a few songs. Bill Black will be here, he's in the Wranglers too. You know Bill Black, Elvis?"

"I know the family," I said. "His brother Johnny is a friend of mine. We've played together."

"Well, when can you come over? I'm here on Belz near Firestone."

"How about tomorrow?" I didn't have the guts to say "right now."

Scotty said, "Tomorrow's the Fourth of July. But, OK, why not, I don't have nothing planned anyhow. How about the afternoon, say two o'clock? Bill should be up by then."

"I'll be there," I said. "Just give me the address."

It was a good omen having the audition on the Fourth of July. I always liked the Fourth. The fireworks. I was a pyromaniac at heart, I swear. Anyhow, I drove over to Scotty's tighter than a tick. It was worse in some ways than auditioning for Sam Phillips cause it was other musicians. My heart was pounding walking up the steps to Scotty's apartment.

Bobbie answered the door. Man, I must've been an eyeful. She probably thought Barnum and Bailey hit town. I was in my pink pants with black tuxedo stripes, jet-black shirt, and white buck shoes. You could of sliced bread with my D.A. There was a heat wave and the pomade on my hair felt like a week-old brownie. I had my little Gene Autry guitar under my arm, not even a case.

"Good afternoon, ma'am. How are you? I'm Elvis Presley. Is Scotty Moore in? This is the right place, isn't it, ma'am?"

Bobbie looked me up and down like I was something out of a cartoon. Later, she told me what she thought about this first time. She said, "I thought you were wearing some kinda Fourth of July costume. Then I thought, hold on a second girl, this ain't Halloween. People don't wear costumes on the Fourth of July!"

She invited me in and went to get Scotty. It looked like a musician's house. Records and song charts were stacked up on the coffee table next to Scotty's chair, beside it were a bunch of country albums, mostly Merle Travis and Chet Atkins, and a new stereo. The portables with detachable speakers had just come in. Scotty walked in and we shook hands. He wasn't big but he was all muscle. Wiry. He had a sly little grin like an elf. Scotty looked me over but he didn't care how I looked. I could of been the Pillsbury Doughboy and it wouldn't of mattered a bit to Scotty.

Bobbie went to get Bill Black, he only lived a few

doors away. Scotty and me chatted a little bit. Even his Levi's and T-shirt was ironed. Scotty was very neat and orderly. He'd just gotten out of the Navy and was working for his brother's dry cleaner blocking hats. He wasn't much for talking but he was a good communicator; Scotty didn't say something unless he thought it out. He asked me about the gigs I'd done. I was honest with him. Told him I sang for friends, couple lodge dances, and that was about it.

Then Bill Black arrived. Through the front window I saw him walking across the lawn, laughing out loud, and he was all by hisself! That was Bill Black though, he was loose.

Scotty let him in. Bill and me shook hands and then he turned to Scotty and said, "Who's his tailor, man? We oughta get him on our party list." Scotty just grinned and looked at the floor.

Bill filled up a room like a dancing bear, he was a born ham. He took a couple of steps back to size me up, put his hands in front of his face like he was about to snap a picture. He says, "It's good, I like it, a singer should stand out. If people mistake you for a popsicle that's their problem." He's standing there telling me all this cracking up. Either you liked Bill or you felt like punching him out. I liked him, at least most of the time.

I said, "I think we met one time over at Charlie's Music. You were coming from a gig and it was late. I was with your brother, Johnny, and he introduced us. "

"Maybe. You're not the kind of guy somebody'd forget though. How do you know Johnny?"

"From the Courts. Johnny lived in the building across the mall, I know your mom and dad."

"When did you move into the Courts, Elvis?"

"Let's see ... it would of been 1949." I was happy to make a little small talk, it calmed me down. You had to like Bill. He was as friendly as a Saint Bernard.

"I left for the service in '46," he said. "Just visited the Courts after that. I must of missed you."

"Yeah. I don't remember ever seeing you there."

Scotty said, "What do you all say we play some songs?" Bill grabbed his acoustic bass from the wall. It was an ol' scuff bucket but it was Bill's mojo; he kept it at Scotty's, that's where the Starlight Wranglers practiced. "What's everybody know?" Scotty said. "How 'bout something by Merle Travis, or maybe Billy Eckstine. Or the Ink Spots."

"Yeah," I said, "either one. Do you all know 'My Happiness'?" I wanted to stick to ballads, tread lightly on the race music, the blues. I was feeling them out.

"Can't say that I do, Elvis." Bill said. "How 'bout Billy Eckstine's, 'I Apologize.'"

We tried to sing it but I was too nervous and it came out forced. My leg was shaking so much it could of been tapped as a new source of energy for the TVA. Basically I was desperate, that's how much I wanted to sing with a band.

"You all know 'I Love You Because'?" I said. Scotty and Bill nodded. We hit it dead on for a minute, and then we pooped-out. I was trying to sing, and that never works, it's gotta come out natural.

Scotty said, "Let's do some Ink Spots. We all know some of those. How 'bout 'Tomorrow'?" It was the same story. I was wired as a cat in a seafood store. My tenor was flying alto. I thought, I better come up with something quick or these guys'll forget about me.

I took a bathroom break and combed my hair. It looked like somebody else in the mirror — much older and half-crazy — your mind does funny things when you're desperate.

We played for a long while, talking half the time: who'd done what and to whom. Memphis, at this time, was a small town musically speaking. We all knew people in common. We got down to a Dean Martin version of Jo Stafford's "You Belong to Me" and I think everybody knew it was time to quit.

I knew I hadn't impressed them much, but there was a lot I was holding back. I didn't want to get into the blues, let alone rhythm and blues. It was just the politics of the time. I had to feel them out first. Much later on they told me what they'd thought: I could sing a little bit, but other than that, they didn't know. That, and I dressed weird.

We got done jamming and I got up to go. Scotty said, "I'll give Sam a call and we'll see what happens. Can you get together again, keep on working it a little bit? Sometimes it takes a while."

I said, "Sure, let's see what we can do." I wasn't worried. I thought he'd call before a week. But that same night, the Fourth of July, Sam Phillips called me. He said, "Let's get some things on tape, see how you boys sound together. Can you do it tomorrow night, Elvis?"

I said, "Sure." This was the best Fourth of July I ever had. Rest of the night I was a Roman candle.

At work the next day I was on cloud nine. Driving up Poplar I saw this sea-green Buick convertible and thought, who knows, maybe I'll be driving something like that soon. My fantasies were open full-throttle. I drove around Mid-town with all the beautiful homes and imagined having everything I wanted. It's good to dream, good thoughts anchor success in your body.

e   *e*   *e*

Sam was getting things ready when I arrived. Scotty and Bill hadn't shown up yet. I played the piano a little, hunt and pecked "Peace in the Valley." Sam was surprised I could play. Scotty and Bill arrived at exactly seven o'clock. I was glad to see them.

"How you all?" Scotty said, "Lord, it's hot. Must of been 120 degrees today at the cleaners. I was drenched all day. It's cool here compared." He shook hands with Sam and me. His eyes were level and clear, Scotty didn't put on airs. I wondered if we'd be friends and thought, it all depends on the music, that's what'll decide things.

Bill smoked a cigarette and tuned up his bass, blowing the ash with the cig still in his mouth. "It was like boot camp in Firestone," Bill said. "All you needed for hell was some witches. Day like today, if they were humane, they close the factory down; that, or serve everybody mint juleps — that'd be OK." He laughed so hard the cigarette fell out of his mouth. He picked it up and kept puffing away.

"I was lucky, I got off work early," I said.

Bill said, "Just wait awhile, Elvis, they'll have you crawling around attics pulling wire on days like this." The three of us were getting on OK. I didn't wanna push myself on anybody.

Sam turned to me and asked, "What do you feel like singing, Elvis?" Scotty and Bill waited for my answer.

I said, "How 'bout 'Harbor Lights'? It wasn't half-bad yesterday."

Scotty said, "What shall we sing it in, Elvis?"

"How 'bout D-minor same as yesterday, let's just keep it simple." I could tell Sam was watching me to see how

I handled myself. I thought, the music'll decide things, nothing else is gonna make a difference.

"You all get started," Sam said, "and I'll set up the mikes and test the levels."

The sweat was dripping off us. It'll be better when the sun goes down and it's night, I thought.

I knew "Harbor Lights" pretty well, I'd been practicing it for years. People make so much of my music, so what I don't understand is why nobody mentions my whistling on "Harbor Lights." It might not of been "The High and the Mighty" but I think it's pretty good, matter of fact, I think a lot of my problems in life would of plumb disappeared if I'd only whistled more!

We did a bunch of takes of "Harbor Lights." Sam kept telling us, "Keep it simple boys, don't try to do too much." We were in the throes of coming together as a band, and that's always a learning process. I kept trying to fit my breath and phrasing with Scotty and Bill. It was tough to control my voice on the ballads, the slow numbers; it took years for me to work up to something like "Love Me Tender."

Listen to "Harbor Lights," you can hear my voice slip higher and higher and then I pull myself back like a balloon. Sam had the patience of Job, we struggled for a couple of hours on the song. "Do it again from the top," he kept saying, "and don't try so hard. Let it come, boys."

Finally he said, "Let's move on to something else. We can come back to 'Harbor Lights' if we need to. What do you wanna do next, Elvis? You got any ideas, Scotty?"

Scotty said, "We did 'I Love You Because' yesterday. We could try that, if Elvis wants to."

I said, "OK." Bill Black looked bored. We have to make something happen, I thought, "Harbor Lights" isn't setting anybody on fire.

We couldn't do anything with "I Love You Because." The record's pretty bad, one of my worst. You can hear how I don't feel the lyrics, I'm all in my head. If you wanna hear me struggle on a song, go listen to it.

Then listen to the difference between "I Love You Because" and "That's Alright Mama." You can see how much I needed a band. I was young and inexperienced and needed other musicians, rhythm and a beat, to channel my voice. I couldn't hold the dynamism of my voice inside the ballads at this time.

I was depressed. We'd been working a couple of hours and hadn't put out a thing. I took a bathroom break to comb my hair.

In the bathroom, I put my head against the wall and said a prayer. I asked for help and for what I should do. Then I heard Jessie speak to me in my heart. "You're acting like you don't count, Elvis. Like you're a beggar at the back door."

I said, right out loud, "I don't know what you're talking about. I'm just trying to make this audition."

"You're not being yourself, that's the only problem you got."

"What do you mean?"

"You're not singing your own music. Where's the songs you love, the blues and the spirituals?"

"I'm waiting till the right time. Is that wrong? I don't wanna push things too quick."

"It's fear, Elvis, that's why you're waiting."

"You think so?"

"You're afraid, aren't you?"

"Yes, I am." I stopped talking out loud. I could hear Jessie better in the quiet of my heart. I thought, should I forget about fear? Let it go and give it to the Lord?

He agreed. "That's what you need to do."

I went back into the studio. Scotty and Bill were relaxing, drinking Cokes and shooting the breeze. I felt myself breathe for the first time all evening. Sam Phillips had his back turned in the control room. He was fooling with the dials on the tape machine. I picked up my guitar and did the blues line of "That's Alright Mama." Bill Black looked up and said, "What's that you're picking? Sounds like some blues."

"Yeah," I said, "it's Big Boy Crudup. 'That's Alright Mama.'"

Bill nodded his head up and down. He had a small smile like an angel's. Scotty looked at me with eyes a million years old.

I started singing kinda falsetto, you know — playing the fool and clowning around and dancing a little. Understand here, we were still on a break. I took "That's Alright Mama" up-tempo to rhythm and blues. I was joking with it, letting myself be a black blues singer. It wasn't anything different than I'd done hundred times for my friends or by myself. Bill Black picked up his bass and started thumping a bass line. He was having a great ol' time whacking that thing like a jungle drum and riding it around. Scotty strapped on his guitar like he was Clark Kent changing to Superman, held that axe like a lightning bolt. We fell in together and really cooked, I mean some mean rhythm and blues. It was rock 'n' roll but nobody knew what to call it.

Sam Phillips heard us in the control room. He said, "What are you boys doing?" He looked like a four-year-old waking up Christmas morning. All three of us at once said, "We don't know."

"Do it again, back it up boys, and see if you can find it. Just take it from the top." Through the window he fiddled with the dials like a mad scientist.

We kept laying down tracks, but it was there from the start. It's always that way with a hit. If you get a song's flow, it seems like it's been with you forever. You don't make a song, you discover it; it's like Columbus finding the New World.

That's how we got started: three white boys, sitting on a mountain of African tinder and scared to death to light the match. I thought it was an accident, but when things are ready, God'll make you the match.

Red Hot and Blue

Sam Phillips played the tape of "That's Alright Mama" and we gathered around to listen to it. It was way past midnight. He said, "It's a hit, boys, listen to that, it's got a bite to it! It's original. People are gonna love it." The three of us looked at each other and shrugged our shoulders. I was excited that Sam was excited, but I didn't get that the song was a hit.

"It's different, I gotta say that," Scotty said. "Now the only question is whether they'll tar and feather us or ride us out of town on a rail." It was the race thing, people were gonna think we were black.

"Don't worry about it," Sam said, "it's fresh, it's different, times are changing. Folks'll listen to this, you'll see."

"It just sounds so ragged and raw, like a jail break," Bill said. "What do you think, Elvis?"

"I don't know," I said, "I think I like it. People are

gonna wonder about it, but maybe that's a good thing. I like how it moves. It's got a beat."

I said goodnight to Scotty and Bill. Sam stayed behind in the studio listening to the tape. He sat there for a couple of hours trying to think of all the reasons why "That's Alright Mama" wouldn't be a hit. But every time he played the tape, he thought, it's a hit, I know it is.

Next morning I was back at work, 7 a.m. at Crown Electric, same as usual. Sam Phillips might of thought we had a hit, but my wallet still looked flatter than the Delta. It was all so unbelievable, it felt like I'd slipped between the sheets of somebody else's life. I told Gladys and Jim Tipler, the owners of Crown, we'd made a record. At first they thought I was kidding them — then they got excited and wanted to know everything. But I didn't feel like talking much, thought it might jinx things. Besides, if I fell flat on my face I didn't want it to be from the penthouse.

Sam had us back in the studio that night, and the one after, too. Worked all kinds of stuff, blues and ballads, but nothing clicked. That was OK, I reckoned Sam would have me around for a couple more weeks no matter what happened. I loved going into the studio every night. Didn't feel like work at all.

On Thursday Sam called me after work. He said Dewey Phillips would probably play the record that night on his show. I took a deep breath and thought, everybody's gonna hear me now. Momma was flying high, she called the whole family and told them I was gonna be on the Dewey Phillips Show. I didn't know whether to take a bow or crawl in a hole. I thought people were gonna laugh at me: "What's an Elvis Presley? Does this guy think he can sing?" I was too nervous to stay home and listen. I set the radio and told my mom and dad to listen. I went to the movies with my cousin Gene.

The Suzores had a Red Skelton comedy, *The Great Diamond Robbery*, but I couldn't keep my mind on the plot. I kept wondering when Dewey Phillips was gonna play the record. I just wanted to get it over with. I reckoned he'd play the record once and that'd be it. I'd go back to being nobody. The second movie just come on, it was a Gene Autry in *Goldtown Ghost Riders*, when I heard my name being called. It was Momma, she was up the aisle hollering, "Elvis, Elvis Presley." I turned around and saw Daddy too — he was going up the other aisle searching for me. I thought, the news must be good, they wouldn't come all the way over to the theater to tell me nobody liked my record.

I stood up and Momma spotted me. She had a grin on her face that went all the way to Little Rock. "Come quick, Elvis," she said, "Dewey Phillips just called the house. He wants to talk to you, right now, on his show! He said, 'get that cotton-picking son of yours over here right now, Mrs. Presley. Everybody wants to hear from the boy.'" I had to scrape her off the theater ceiling, she was going a mile a minute. "He's playing the record over and over again, honey. People are calling in."

Daddy stood next to her and smiled. He didn't say a word.

I said, "I'll go home right now and give him a call."

"No, honey, Dewey said not on the phone. He wants you to come to the station and be interviewed on the air. He said folks are ringing the phone off the hook, even sending telegrams. I couldn't believe it — them saying your name over the radio — 'Elvis Presley.' This is a new song by 'Elvis Presley.' I thought, Lord, I'm dreaming. He kept playing the song over and over. It's been on ten times, I swear. Lord in Heaven, this is the most exciting thing that's ever happened. Dewey said to get you quick, so your daddy and me came right over."

I said, "I guess I should just go over to the station then, it's only a couple of blocks away."

My cousin Gene had gotten up and was standing next to me in the aisle. He said, "Let's go, man," and pointed at the screen, "You can visit with these cows anytime."

There were a lot of folks on the street. It was hot and people were out for an evening stroll. It was a Thursday night. We walked fast; the Chisca Hotel, where Dewey broadcast from, was a half-a-dozen blocks up Main Street. Memphis seemed small like Tupelo. I saw folks in their apartments, peoples' lights were just coming on, and wondered if any of them were listening to "That's Alright Mama." People were hearing me on their radios. I was in shock, lightheaded: it felt like the whole world was pouring into my heart. I gave thanks to God.

We slowed down and Gene said, "I gotta a feeling, Elvis, this could be a night we remember forever."

"I don't wanna think about it, Gene," I said. I was afraid to speak of it. "What's Dewey Phillips gonna ask me on the radio?" I said. "Hope he don't ask me about how we came up with the song. I can't even remember."

"He'll probably ask about yourself."

"What do you mean, like where I was born or what?"

"I have no idea. Just about your life, could be anything. Like where you went to school. Who knows, man, don't worry about it. He wouldn't be talking to you if people weren't interested. Tell 'em anything, make something up."

"Sure, easy for you to say, you're gonna be standing there laughing at me. Maybe I should tell them I was raised-up in France, by gypsies, or better yet, I came from another planet." We cracked up.

Gene said, "I'll tell you one thing, Elvis, right about now I'd sure trade places with you, buddy." He didn't want me to leave him, I saw it in his eyes.

We got to the entrance of the Chisca Hotel. There were a couple of doormen out front looking like admirals in the Royal Navy. I felt like asking them for permission to board, but as we stepped forward they threw the doors wide open. The lobby was filled with people. I looked up to the mezzanine, that's where Dewey had his show. I reckoned I didn't have anything important enough to say over the radio, but what the heck, they wanted to talk to me.

Gene and me bounded up the stairs, three steps at a time. We were in a big-time hotel with business to do! We walked into the studio and Dewey was on the air. He caught me out of the side of his eye and waved. For some reason he knew who I was. Later I asked him about it, how he knew it was me. He said, "You looked like you belonged, son. Like you were a star."

He motioned for me to come in the control room and sit down. I took the seat beside him. He was younger than I thought and his eyes were kind. He was playing "That's Alright Mama" and talking over it.

"Call your ol' lady from the kitchen, get grandma and little sister too, they're gonna love the boy sitting down next to me here. Wait till you women see how this boy looks! Oh yeah! I'm telling you guys, hold on to Myrtle and don't let go, the womenfolk gonna have to be tied down when they get a load of this cat. Oh yeah, I got Elvis. Elvis Presley is sitting right here next to me. What kinda name Elvis be? Well, we'll all find out cause he's gonna tell us everything he knows, and what he don't know too. Lemme get this beer commercial out the way and we'll have the man of the hour ... the week ... the century — who knows! — just call Myrtle, she ain't gonna wanna miss Elvis Presley. "

My head spun. It was one thing hearing Dewey over the radio, but in person the man was a human tornado.

Dewey played a commercial. "Glad to meet you, Elvis," he said, and we shook hands. "They love your song, man, won't lemme stop playing it. It's gonna be a hit, you'll see. If it's OK I wanna talk to you on the air, let people know who you are. Everybody wants to meet you, man; they're sending over telegrams, pigeons, and pony express. They think you're Negro. People aren't gonna believe their ears. Be sure to tell 'em you went to Humes High, that way people'll know you're white. Now when I talk to you don't say nothing dirty. This is a family show and we got to keep it clean, you know what I mean." He poked me in the ribs and laughed. You couldn't help but love Dewey, he was so outrageous.

"No sir," I said, "I sure won't say anything dirty. I'll make sure of that." Like I was about to blow my big chance by telling dirty jokes. I thought, how does Dewey know I went to Humes? Then I reckoned it was Sam Phillips who told him. I was a little scared him saying I sounded Negro. I didn't know what was gonna happen.

Dewey went back at it, pounding the table for CV Beer. "Tomorrow's Friday, pay day and bath day; I got a letter from grandma, she's boogeying all night long with CV Beer. I just swallowed my gold tooth, folks, hold a second while I call my dentist, or maybe I should call a proctologist. Anybody know a good one? CV Beer, it's got the champagne-velvet taste, pick up a case or three, tell those Huskies mush and crash through the saloon doors, have yourself a party.

"Pop one open right now; let's have the man making all the mamas feel alright, yes sir, Mr. Elvis Presley, here right now."

"We on the air?" I said.

Dewey put his hand over the mike and whispered, "No, not yet. Lemme get some information on you, son, so I'll know what to talk to the folks about."

Dewey asked me, "How long you been singing, Elvis?"

"Longtime, I guess. When I was ten years old my momma got me a guitar for my birthday. I wanted a rifle but she said I had to take the guitar. This was in Tupelo. It was quite a long time ago, sir."

"What kind of music you like, this here's a blues song, 'That's Alright Mama.' Yes sir, Mr. Big Boy Crudup. Is that the kind of music you like, Elvis, the blues?"

"Sure. I like the blues. I like all kinds of music, sir, country, pop, blues. If it's music I like it, I guess."

"Where'd you go to school, son? Was it here in town? You been here for awhile, right?"

"Yes, sir. I graduated from Humes High School right here in Memphis. It's on Manassas. Probably some of the people listening in went to Humes. That's where I graduated, sir, last year, 1953."

"You a singer now? What kind of work you do?

"Well, I'm driving a truck now, sir. I work for Crown Electric over on Poplar. Gladys and Jim Tipler, they been very nice to me. I'm going to school to be an electrician, so I just hope I don't electrocute myself."

"You gonna make any more records, Elvis? Is that what you're gonna do?"

"I hope so. That's sure what I want. If I can do it I will. I guess it's what people want. They want some records, I'll do it. That's what I'm hoping for." I was wondering when the interview was gonna start cause I was getting nervous about what to say. I asked Dewey, "When we gonna start the interview?"

"We done it, son. You been on the air. You did great."

I didn't know whether to hug him or hit him, but that was Dewey Phillips.

The whole night was a dream, like it was happening to somebody else. And it did in a way, my life changed after this night, things were never the same.

I walked home with Gene and we said goodbye. My Dad met me at the door. He said, "I'm proud of you, son." His eyes were sad even though he was smiling. This got to be a ritual with us over the years, his saying he was proud of me. There was always a little bit of sadness in him that I could never figure out. I understand now. There was so much he wanted to say but couldn't. That was the sadness.

Momma, on the other hand, was bubbling over — she didn't hold nothing back when she was happy. Soon as I got in, she wanted to feed me of course.

"Sit down now, Elvis, I got new cornbread for you. Your Daddy and me heard you on the radio, but we gotta know everything that happened with Dewey. We gotta hear it all, isn't that right, Vernon? You wanna soak your cornbread, Elvis? I got a new bottle of buttermilk, sweetheart."

They made me tell them over and over about being on Dewey's show, they wanted to hear it from me.

Wishing on the Moon

Sam Phillips was chomping at the bit for a "B" side for "That's Alright Mama." He wanted a country number to balance out the blues, it was a political thing, a country song with a blues number would help white folks get comfortable with the race music.

It took a few days but we came up with something, again just by accident. We weren't smart enough to do something intentionally. We were on a break same as "That's Alright Mama," when Bill Black started riding his bass around the studio, acting the fool on Bill Monroe's tune, "Blue Moon of Kentucky." Scotty and me grabbed our guitars and jumped in, taking Monroe's waltz to a fast trot. We turned "Blue Moon of Kentucky," a bluegrass song, into rhythm and blues.

Sam Phillips shot up from his seat in the control room and ran into studio, waving his arms like a brakeman on the railroad. "Don't change anything, just take it from the top, boys. Lemme get this on tape." It was one big accident same as "That's Alright Mama"; that's how "Blue Moon of Kentucky" was born.

With any song you gotta find a way inside it and feel how *it* wants to be. A song can have a lot of moods too. Our "Blue Moon of Kentucky" is a rhythm blast with the guitars holding the beat. But it was the lyrics that made the song. "Blue Moon of Kentucky" is about a guy who's lost his girl and wants the moon to bring her back, and wishing on the moon was right up my alley, that's what put my voice in overdrive on the record. It's a real throttle-burner — a cruising song.

We had a record and after all the years of dreaming I *had* to be there to see it pressed. I got the morning off work and went to Buster Williams' Plastics with a high school buddy, Ed Leeks. You woulda thought it was Ed's record he was so pumped up.

We got there as Buster was setting up. How a voice ended up on grooves of vinyl was a mystery to me. Buster tried to explain it, but I couldn't make heads or tails of it. I was too excited. They got all the machines cued up and then it didn't work. Buster and his men fiddled for a while, then they gave me the high sign. I saw my first record punched and slide out. Didn't have a label or anything. The records kept plopping out like eggs from a hen. I guess the whole thing mesmerized me cause when I looked up everybody in the room was looking at me. I was grinning so much it was embarrassing. Everybody gave me a hand, right then and there. I felt like crying.

On the way home Ed and me cruised by Leonard's to see if anybody was around. We pulled in and spotted a few cars we knew. Word was getting around about the record after the Dewey Phillips' show. I ordered four cheeseburgers and a double chocolate shake. Gave myself a stomachache. I was on top of the world though.

The record was in the stores right away. Sun #209. I liked the ring of it — number 209 — sounded like a hit. Numbers always fascinated me. Later on I studied numerology which is the cosmic aspect of numbers. Divine light sequences itself by number, but that's a whole other matter.

Every day for awhile I went over to Charlie's Music and Poplar Tunes to see my record in the bins. Charlie Hazelwood put it on the jukebox. If somebody bought the record while I was there I signed it. I was amazed folks were paying good money for my record. It takes awhile for fame and fortune to sink in, and it's too bad when it does. Never had as much fun selling my records as in the beginning. I was as stoked that first day Poplar Tunes sold a hundred of "That's Alright Mama" as anytime I went platinum.

We got some gigs around town. First one was at a red-neck bar on Summer, the Bon Air. It was a Saturday night. The Bon Air was a pretty rough place. We used to joke that "Bon Air" was French for that delightful rising of the male species. Didn't matter whether it was testosterone or beer, the Bon Air was a tough crowd used to meat-and-potatoes country music. I didn't know but they'd take offense to what we'd done to Bill Monroe's "Blue Moon of Kentucky," let alone us singing race music. I imagined a bunch of disgruntled cowboys cooking up a batch of tar and feathers for yours truly. I was glad family and friends came to the show, I'll tell you that.

Nothing bad happened at all. People like good music no matter what it is. They ended up cheering us.

The record was getting air time too, and not just in Memphis. Disc jockeys in New Orleans and Texas jumped on it, thanks to Sam. The man was working 28 hours day making things snowball. Point of fact, our first big record order came out of Texas. That was a portent of things to come. Texas was where things really got rocking. Our first big gig was at the Overton Park Shell in Memphis. It was a Slim Whitman show and the house was gonna be a couple thousand. This was the big time, man, didn't even matter they got my name wrong on the posters. I guess they reckoned nobody would actually be named Elvis Presley so they called me Ellis. I thought it was kinda distinctive, you know, Ivy League.

By the day of the show I coulda been the "before" advertisement for pharmaceutical tranquilizers. One minute I imagined myself as sensational, and the next, I was worried about even singing. What scared me most was people having no response — we'd get up on stage and it'd be the like the day the Earth stood still. That one gave me cold sweats.

It was an eight o'clock show on a Friday night, July the 30th, 1954, to be exact. We were the warm-up for Slim Whitman and Billy Walker, it was a country and western jamboree put on by Bob Neal, who later became my manager.

I drove over to Overton Park with Dixie. There was some tension between us cause of all the attention I was getting, particularly from the girls. She could see I was getting off on it. But then again, who wouldn't of? No girlfriend wants to see that, though. I didn't wanna break up and date other girls, but I couldn't say the idea hadn't crossed my mind.

I said, "What's going on, you're kinda quiet, Dixie." She looked beautiful sitting next to me in a yellow sun dress. Her hair was red in the sunlight and it curled over the little string straps on her shoulders. I did love her, it's just that I was torn.

"I don't know, Elvis, everybody's gonna be making over you tonight, and they should, it's your night." She held her purse over her stomach and looked straight ahead. "I don't know where I fit in, I guess. You're the one who's the star, Elvis."

My first thought was always, what can I do to patch things up? I said, "This here's a Slim Whitman show. He's the star, that's who people are coming to see, Dixie. I'm just gonna be there, it's a chance for us to practice in front of a big crowd. That's why Sam Phillips set it up. If we're gonna get good we gotta do stuff like this, but I'm not a star." I was making excuses, even at this point.

"You're gonna be. Everytime you play, Elvis, people love you. You don't see it but you're gonna be a star, that's just the way it is. And you know how the girls are with a singer. You pretend like you don't, but you do. Like last night at Leonard's. Every girl in the place was over at our car when you got your guitar out."

She kinda had me. I knew what was happening with the girls — and I liked it. "Nobody's gonna be making over me," I lied. "I'll be lucky if I ever play this big a show again. I'll probably be playing at honky-tonks in West Memphis after this. Sweeping the places out. Nothing's gonna happen, Dixie." I didn't know what else to do but joke things off.

"You're gonna be a star, you'll see. You just don't want to admit it and I'm not sure why. Probably cause you don't want to lose me. But the truth's the other way around, Elvis — I'm the one who doesn't wanna lose you."

At the stage door we said goodbye and Dixie went to look for my mom and dad. Nobody was backstage yet except for a couple of stagehands, so I wandered behind the Shell and sat down under a sycamore tree. I saw the Memphis Zoo across the way and remembered the time I went with my Uncle Noah, when I was nine years old. He took a bunch of us kids on the East Tupelo school bus. It was a great day, I saw an anaconda big enough to swallow a cow, and the chimpanzees tried to spit on us. It was the funniest thing you'd ever seen.

Sam found me, he was wearing a Panama hat and cream-colored slacks. I was happy to see him. He saw how nervous I was. "How you doing son?" he said, "Getting ready for the show back here, huh?"

"I wanna thank you for all you've done for me, Mr. Phillips. I wouldn't even be here without you." I squirmed in my new shoes trying to get my feet comfortable. "I hope I don't mess everything up for you and Mr. Neal."

Sam shook his head and laughed. "Elvis, you gotta remember, son, this is just the start of things. Even if you do screw up, and you won't, we're still OK. Wouldn't change things a bit, trust me. What's the record been out? Not even three weeks and it's getting played all over town. Show these people what you got and everything'll take care of itself, I guarantee it." He put his hand on my shoulder. "Don't worry about nothing, leave it all up to me." He walked back to the Shell through the shadows of the poplars and sycamores. I should trust him, I thought, he's the one who knows the music business.

The Shell filled up and I got stage fright. It's a miserable disease, stage fright, you never really kick it. There was at least two thousand people this night, it was standing room. Slim Whitman had a big following from the Louisiana Hayride and "Indian Love Call," and Billy Walker had a new hit out, "Thank You for Calling." And then there was the folks who came to see us.

We came on before Slim Whitman, Bob Neal introduced us. "Let's have a big Memphis cheer for our local boys," he said. People down front jumped up and cheered. "They got a new record out and you all know it's doing good. These boys here are Elvis Presley, Scotty Moore, and Bill Black, and they're gonna sing you the songs right now." I saw my Mom and Dixie, and my Dad, down in front. Momma was wearing the corsage I bought her. I looked up at the moon and took a deep breath. It was full.

My knees were shaking like a pair of castanets. Scotty and Bill were scared too. This was by far the biggest house they'd played. It was a big oval stage and we were out there like three little lost sheep. I'd waited my whole life for this night, and now it had come. I stepped up to the mike to adjust it and nearly twisted the sucker off, that's how amped I was.

I said, "We're gonna sing a song for you we just recorded for Sun Records, it's called 'That's Alright Mama.'" Cheers went up around the Shell, I felt like I'd been put in a jar with a storm. I sang the rhythm lead-in to "That's Alright Mama" ... *Ta dee da dee dee da*. Folks knew the song, they were singing along with me. The lights in the tall trees bathed the crowd in yellow-green light. We hit the song dead-on, caught its flow like the curl of a wave, the moon above glowed silver behind the clouds. I felt big inside my clothes and my arms and legs felt like satin. They're pulling for us, I thought, they want us to do good.

I pulled back from the mike and played, moving and dancing to the music a little bit. I jiggled my leg and heard people holler, Scotty looked over at me with big eyes. I did it more and got the same reaction as the Chief, the girls started screaming. I was wearing baggy pants so it looked like there was a whole lot more going on in there than there was. But what the heck, that's show business.

We got done with "That's Alright" and the crowd let loose. People stood and clapped. We had 'em, we were in.

We did "Blue Moon of Kentucky" and it turned into a party. Bill rode his bass around the stage like Trigger, one hand raised in the air and the other thumping away. Bill wasn't the best bass player in the world, and he had more fun than anybody. Scotty Moore flat broke the song down, he had some great riffs on "Blue Moon of Kentucky." Scotty doesn't get the credit he deserves. He was a big part of our sound. I let myself go and shook all over.

We took our bow and folks hollered, "Encore! Encore!" We hadn't talked about an encore, the thought never crossed our minds. I looked offstage to Slim Whitman and Bob Neal. Slim smiled and motioned with his hands for us to go ahead. Bob Neal looked at Slim and then at us. He nodded his head up and down. We only knew two songs. We did "Blue Moon of Kentucky" again. The crowd loved it even more.

Slim Whitman came on, the gracious gentleman he was, and said, "How you gonna do better than that?"

We got off stage and Sam was beaming. It was a great night, the record had gotten a big boost. He took us aside in back of the Shell underneath the trees. There was a bright light above us. He said, "You all were great, now we gotta keep it up. Tomorrow every disc jockey in town's gonna be on the record. That'll boot sales right up, which'll lead to more radio, then there'll be more shows and more sales, that's how it spirals. I talked to Biff Collie this afternoon in Houston. He asked if you boys wanted to play The Magnolia Gardens in a few weeks.

"But you need more songs, so you gotta keep practicing; you get three or four songs out and you can talk to the Louisiana Hayride, or even the Opry. I'm hitting the road with the record Sunday night, I'll talk to all the distributors again. It's all possible boys, you just gotta keep working. Practice, every day, and learn some more songs."

e　　　　　*e*　　　　　*e*

One night a few weeks later, after working at the studio, Sam and I went over to his house. It was late and his wife and kids were asleep. We sat out on the patio. Sam had a beautiful place with tall trees and a garden with lighted paths. Sam brought me a Coke and took down a bottle of Jack Daniels and two shooters. He knew I didn't drink but he always put out a glass for me. It was the middle of the night and the heat was still thick.

I knew he'd grown up in Alabama, near Muscle Shoals, but this night he talked about his childhood with me. Sam's father died when he was in high school; after that, he was the one responsible for his mother and deaf aunt. He told me about his family's plantation in Florence and how he was the youngest of eight. He'd been sickly as a child and the black folks on the farm had looked after him, in particular an old man there he called Uncle Silas. Silas Payne. Silas loved young Sam and told him all the old African tales. They'd sit under a live oak by the creek that ran around the house and Uncle Silas would play the guitar and sing his stories. Sam would close his eyes and see the molasses rivers and trees of eternal fruit that Uncle Silas sang about. Music called Sam, like it had me. He heard the black folks singing in the fields, the call and answer as they hoed the cotton. His heart felt pierced by it.

As he got older, Sam wanted to be strong and brave like his big brother, Jud. Everybody loved Jud, and Sam wanted to be just like him. But Sam was sickly, and he was left home when the men went out to work or to ride the horses. He cured himself of his illness by an act of will. He decided he was through with it — wouldn't pay the sickness any mind or accept the goodwill of others — he rose up against it and smote it down. I wasn't much different. With me it was poverty, though.

As Sam talked, his head tipped back with that salty chuckle of his. He laughed up at the stars. "The soul of man abides in Negro music, Elvis." Sam pointed above. "People find what they're looking for. Hey, there's Orion's Belt right above us!"

People find what they're looking for. Sam was right, people see what they wanna see. The night around us felt fat, chock-full of life, the crickets and frogs roared, and I heard the slither of little critters amongst the leaves.

220.

Sam said, "First time I saw Beale Street I was home, not that I was gonna go live in the ghetto, Elvis … but I don't know, maybe that would be fun; it was the feeling the brothers had, not the dandies in their zoot suits, but the Negroes who'd just come up-country, the guys off plantations with mud on their boots and voices to break your heart. Singing on street corners, or in the park, for nickels in a hat, Robert Johnsons, and nobody had ever heard them."

"I know what you mean," I said. "I go to the Palace Theater — when I don't have the money I stand outside the doors — the lights of Beale Street, people going in and out of Pantaze Drugs or over to Sunbeam Mitchell's. It's the coolest place in town. But people, the white race, ain't ready to understand yet."

Clive East

A few weeks after the Overton Shell concert we did a show that meant a lot to me. It was a benefit for disabled vets at Kennedy Veterans' Hospital in Memphis. A wonderful lady, Mrs. Weiner, set it up under the auspices of B'nai B'rith. She asked if we could come by and play for the paralyzed veterans. They were shut-ins and never got a chance to see music. I really wanted to do it, and so did Scotty and Bill.

This was just after the Korean War, so there were a lot guys at the hospital recovering from war injuries, some since World War II. It was a Saturday afternoon. I got over there early so I'd have a chance to visit with some of the soldiers. I knew how tough the Korean War had been. My cousin Junior Smith, Gene's brother, had come back shell shocked. His wounds were on the inside, psychological, and they were devastating, so I could only imagine what it was like to have an arm or leg blown off. Truth is, it's easy to feel set aside and forgotten in a Veterans Hospital. Most of us forget all too quick the sacrifices that soldiers make for our freedom.

We were downstairs in a little rec room. The place was depressing to tell the truth, I mean the whole hospital. Why do Veterans Hospitals have to be painted in drab colors with floors to match? Let the guys get crazy with finger paints and draw flowers on the wall. People are hurting, their lives smashed, and they're supposed to fit into neat little boxes like pills in a Dixie cup? I know the people in charge are trying, but the institutional mind takes over, which is an oxymoron if there ever was one.

The room was packed tight with wheelchairs and stretchers. I was surprised how many soldiers knew us. They'd heard our record on the radio. They had a lot of time to listen to the radio; these guys knew their music.

We started with "That's Alright Mama" like usual. Everybody was into it from the get-go. Doctors and nurses were standing outside the doors looking in. It was amazing, whatever these vets had of their bodies they were gonna use it to dance. If they could clap to the beat they did, but if they could only move a nose or an eyebrow, or purse their lips, that's what they shook. It was the darndest thing you'd ever seen. I looked out over that sea of soldiers and their joy was a sight to behold. One guy was keeping the beat wiggling his nose and another was getting down syncopating his ears. They were clapping with their faces, and if they were gonna use all of what little they had, I wasn't gonna hold back. I gave 'em the full show, windmills, 360s, the more I shook it up, the higher everybody went. Bill rode his bass and Scotty got up on his tippy-toes reaching for that last row that'd never been plowed. We were men possessed. You might of thought those soldiers felt bad seeing somebody move and shake it; but no, they wanted us to live what they couldn't.

Doesn't matter what you have — it's what you do with it. The secret of happiness is appreciating what you got.

We got done and I was dripping wet. Somebody tossed me a towel. A guy hollered out, "Oh yeah, us gimps getting down," and broke everybody up. One of the soldiers called me over to his chair. "You go to Humes, Elvis?"

"Yeah, I did," I said. "Graduated last year. How 'bout you? You go to Humes?"

"Yes. I graduated in '51, so I was a couple years ahead of you." He was missing his right arm and a foot. "I'm Clive East," he said, "glad to meet you, man. I remember you, but you've changed. You were pretty shy before, seemed like you were always by yourself. What got into you? Whatever it is, lemme know where I can get some."

He was in a bathrobe and pajamas and looked small in the wheelchair. I remembered him. He'd been prematurely bald, but a good looking guy. I wanted to tell him I was sorry for what happened. He took hold of my hand with a strong grip.

"You're gonna be a star," he said. "White folks wanna hear the blues too, you'll see."

"We'll see what comes." I said, "It's fun doing it." I felt guilty standing there with my whole life in front of me. Clive didn't wanna let go of my hand.

"I'm OK," he said, "I'll be getting outta here sooner or later. Hey, when I do, I'm gonna come and see you play. I'll bring my sister along. She'd like you. I'll come backstage maybe, if I can make it."

"Sure," I said, "do that." And he did, about a year later.

There was a circle of wheelchairs and stretchers around me. They were all so young, even the guys who'd been around since World War II. I was a messenger from the world I guess. They wanted news, what clubs we'd played and had we seen this or that act. They gave me a lot of encouragement and wished me well as we shook hands. One guy didn't have a hand to shake. All he had were nubs. I put my hand on his shoulder and he pressed his nubs against my arm.

Me and Scotty and Bill had gone to Kennedy to give the vets something, but they gave us ten back. The days ahead brought criticism; I was called everything from devil-inspired to the Pied Piper of Hootchie-Kootchie for how I moved and danced. I was leading kids astray. I was lewd and sinful. It hurt, but when I felt down, I'd think about the soldiers at Kennedy Hospital.

People and their courage, that's what I think about now. Anybody can be on top if they're getting the Nobel Prize, but how 'bout if you're stuck in a wheelchair or somebody has to feed you. Then you gotta dig deeper to find life.

e   *e*   *e*

A few days after the Kennedy show, I found my momma out on the porch. It was a Sunday afternoon. She was knitting a blanket. "Ain't it too hot for that?" I said, "Knitting blankets in the middle of summer. Who's this one for?" There were two rocking chairs and I sat down beside her.

"I don't know yet," she said, "maybe it'll be a Christmas present. Or maybe I'll give it to you for a wedding present. Dixie's a darling girl, I see the way you two look at each other. Wouldn't surprise me a bit if you came home one morning and said you'd been to Hernando." She was talking about Hernando, Mississippi, anybody over the age of five could elope in Hernando.

"And leave you out, I'd never hear the end of it. Besides I may be travelling soon, doing the music, and I don't know how that mixes with marriage and having kids." This was the first time I brought up touring to her and I was dreading it.

She got quiet and shifted in her chair. "There I go missing a stitch. Where are those glasses of mine?" She rummaged through her purse looking for her spectacles.

She didn't wanna look at me. She was a little girl again, moving from one plantation to another, walking beside the new landlord's wagon filled with the family's stuff. She'd never looked up then either. I felt her, the toughest thing about all the success would be leaving Momma. I thought it might kill her.

"When do you think you'll go, honey?"

"Maybe a couple of weeks. Sam told Scotty there's some shows we might do, in Texas, Gladwater's one place, Lubbock, maybe Houston at the Magnolia Gardens. Maybe it won't happen. But we gotta promote the record and going on the road'll do that."

"You gotta do for your career, Elvis. You can't be worrying about your daddy and me." She was being brave but there was such a sadness in her. It broke my heart.

"I'll talk to you every night on the telephone and tell you about what happened. We're not gonna be gone that much anyhow." She started coughing. It was asthma, undiagnosed. And she couldn't stop coughing. I ran into the kitchen and got her a glass of water and brought it back. She gulped it down and the coughing stopped.

"Maybe you go travelling with your music for a couple years and then you come home."

"Yeah, probably will."

"You'd have the money to open a store, have your own business. That way you wouldn't be answering to anybody, Elvis. You could have your kids then."

"I think the music'll let me help you and Daddy."

"You'll do that, honey, it's just your nature. You've always been sweet, Elvis." My mother was brave. It was the Irish in her.

"I'll help you and Daddy if I can." I'd of done anything for her, except stop the music. It started to rain.

New York

Some turning points you only see after you die, like my first trip to New York City for the Dorsey Brothers' show. Actually it was my second trip to New York; we'd gone up the year before to try out for Arthur Godfrey's Talent Scouts, but it was that first Dorsey trip when I felt the excitement of New York, probably cause I was on the verge of success. New York City is a special place when you know you're on the way up. This was January, 1956.

I was twenty-one. I'd just recorded "Heartbreak Hotel." It was my first recording for RCA, they were worried — they thought it was too depressing — but I never worried about the song from the first time I heard it.

A couple of days before the Dorsey show I flew in from Texas with Colonel Parker. We went over to RCA Victor's headquarters in Manhattan and I got introduced around. I met Larry Kanaga, the head of the record division, and their publicity woman, Anne Fulchino. We shot the breeze for awhile and then went out to lunch at the Russian Tea Room; Steve Sholes, my record producer at Victor, joined us. One thing I gotta say about New York, the food's great and they don't stiff you on the portions.

After lunch it was raining and we scurried back to the RCA building. Anne wasn't much older than me, but she'd made it, at least from the look of her office. She had a big oval window overlooking the City and I sat across from it on a calfskin couch, watching the storm brew through the skyscrapers. It was breathtaking, that's the only word for it, New York is the capital of the world. The City is famous for its tall buildings, of course, but I always sensed the depths of New York — it feels as if a bass note rises from the bowels of it. It's all the minds, and lives, that've inhabited the place, they've rooted New York City deep into the ground. Anne came from behind her desk and sat beside me, scribbling diagrams on a pad of paper. She was a beautiful brunette with curly hair and skin as fresh as new cream. By this time I was used to women coming on to me, but I couldn't read her, not in that way.

Anne said we should follow a game plan step by step so that everything was systematic. She drew pyramid on top of pyramid in her yellow pad, the records set up the concert tours, and the tours sold records. I trusted her, it's what Sam Phillips had said, he saw the big picture too. She didn't mention "Heartbreak Hotel," or any particular record, she just spoke of the hits coming like they were a foregone conclusion. That's how I felt too. It was prophecy being fulfilled.

Anne asked me where I saw myself in two years, and even further out, five or ten years down the line. I didn't know what to say. I didn't want her to think I was egotistical, so I waited for her to talk. She gazed out the window, resting her chin in her hand. Did I see myself making movies, she asked, Frank Sinatra and Bing Crosby had done it, was it something I saw for me? I thought about it all the time. I wanted to be in a movie *with* James Dean. He was portraying the new generation, and that's what I wanted to do too.

All of it scared me, but I didn't let it show. It's what I wanted — the success I mean. I felt like there was two of me, one Elvis on stage blasting peoples' doors off, and the other one afraid it was all coming too quick. I already had a prescription for sleeping pills, I was so hopped up all the time.

We were staying at the Warwick Hotel in Manhattan, near Studio Fifty where the Dorsey Brothers' show was broadcast. The Saturday of the show we rehearsed in the afternoon and then came back to the room to relax and get ready. "Heartbreak Hotel" had been released and we listened to it and a couple of other demos from the Nashville session, "Money Honey" and "I Got A Woman." My cousin Gene was with me, and the rest of the band; Colonel Parker was at the hotel too. I thought about being on TV before the whole country. It was weird, the Colonel said we'd reach as many people with one national TV broadcast as a lifetime of appearances on the Louisiana Hayride, my steady gig on Saturday nights for that past year.

A reporter from a New York newspaper came up to the room. Bright guy, blond hair and wire-rimmed glasses, looked like he could've been a college profes- sor. We talked for a few minutes and then I ran out of things to say. I turned him over to Bill Black; we had a system where Bill would take over with reporters and bs 'em for awhile. It ticked the Colonel off, but we didn't care. Bill'd make up stories about roadhouses and how we'd won over the local populace with the magic of rock 'n' roll. It was a crackup, Bill'd make it sound like I was the Pied Piper.

Bill took over with the reporter and I stretched out on a couch on the other side of the room and read fan let- ters, which was one of my favorite things to do. "Elvis," Bill hollered over to me, "tell this reporter about what happened in Texarkana with your car." He turned to the reporter and said, "You gotta hear this one," and slapped him so hard on the back the guy nearly lost his pad and pen. "Elvis," Bill says, "is so hot he bursts into flames ... from time to time!"

It was a funny story, so I told it again. "We were on tour," I said, "This was last summer, and it was the middle of the night, maybe three or four in the morning, and we were headed down to Texarkana on Highway Sixty-nine. I had a new pink Cadillac, only had it for a couple of months. Bill had crashed my Lincoln that winter — drove it under a hay truck going ninety — so I'd just got this pink Cadillac and it was my dream car. The night I bought it I stayed up till dawn looking at the car outta my hotel window. Anyhow, I'm with a date so Scotty and Bill were following us in another car." The reporter looked at Scotty and Bill, who were covering their mouths from laughing, and wondered how this story of me bursting into flames was gonna turn funny. The guy must have thought he had some psycho-hayseeds on his hands.

I went on with the story. "I heard a loud knock in the front end of the Cadillac, down low in the wheel-well, and my first thought was, it must be a flat. Then smoke started pouring out of the front end and the steering got squirrelly. I pulled over, and it's good thing I did, cause flames started leaping up from the driver's-side wheel-well. The young lady screamed, 'We're on fire! We're on fire!' and by God we were. The flames spread to the engine and the car filled up with smoke.

"I grabbed our guitars out of the trunk and took the young lady's hand and we clambered up the hillside as fast as we could. We were afraid the gas tank was gonna blow. It all happened so fast, it was amazing. I'm up on the hillside looking down in shock, watching my pride and joy, this gorgeous pink Caddy, go up in flames. The car horn was blaring like a cow fixing to deliver a herd of Brahma bulls. It was saddest thing you'd ever seen. I'd worked all year for the car — and now it was up in smoke."

I got done with the story and Bill nearly fell off his chair laughing. Scotty cried he laughed so hard. I know the reporter thought we were completely nuts.

"It was the road that made us crazy. When the Caddy burned-up we were bummed-out; but you go on — to the next town, and the next show — the gigs and the road pile up, after awhile everything's a joke cause you're just plumb rummy. Driving all night to the next town we used to play a game. No matter what you were talking about you had to change the subject when somebody tap-tap-tapped you on the top of your head. I thought we all made more sense, personally.

"Last year, '55, the first six months of the year we drove more than 300,000 miles. I'm not kidding, ask Gene, we figured it out. I'd never been anywhere till we started touring. It was like vacation to me, staying in motels and eating out in restaurants; still, it don't take long before you need a vacation from vacation in the worst way. I'd go to breakfast in the morning and have to ask the waitresses what state I was in. God bless them, they kept their comments to geography."

The reporter scribbled away, he probably thought he'd discovered the secret of why rock 'n' rollers are nuts. My cousin Gene leaned back in his chair at the dining table, watching us. Gene said, "Why don't you tell this reporter what happened in Jacksonville, Elvis. When the girls decided you needed a new paint job."

"Oh yeah," I said, "that was a Friday the 13th. We were doing a show at the Gator Bowl, huge crowd, musta been fourteen, fifteen thousand people. Something got into me, cause as I walked off stage I grabbed the mike and said, 'Girls ... I'll see you all backstage' — and I took off through a baseball dugout into the dressing room. I wasn't in there a minute, when I heard a sound like a herd of rhinos at the windows at the top of the wall. A bunch of girls had taken me at my word and were commencing to pile through the windows, tumbling ass-over-teakettle into the dressing room.

"They got a bead on me and I thought, Oops, I got trouble. These girls didn't even bother with a howdy-doo before they started pawing and grabbing for whatever they could get. There was nowhere to run so I climbed on top of a shower stall and hollered for help. They tore off my jacket and shredded my shirt like confetti. I was laughing but it like to scare me to death, I thought they were gonna tear me apart. The girls were working on my pants when I heard the police chief come in and holler that everybody was under arrest. I reckoned that'd put a stop to it — but the girls kept pawing away — finally, the police got to me before all my decency was removed.

"I wasn't angry — just amazed! — things got outta hand *so* fast. I told the police to let 'em go, the girls hadn't meant any harm. They were clearing the place out when Faron Young spotted this young chick shuffling toward the door looking like the Hunchback of Notre Dame. Faron tripped her and my boots fell out from her back. She'd stuffed 'em under her blouse. So I got my boots back. I got back to my car and it was covered in lipstick with girls' names and telephone numbers. Some of them had carved their numbers in the paint with keys. Had to send the car out to be repainted. Then, like I said, the car burned up a month later."

Everybody laughed. The reporter joined in this time, I guess he reckoned our craziness wasn't all bad. I excused myself to get ready for the show and went into the bathroom.

We were coming up in the world, the towels in the hotel bathrooms were thicker and the soaps had French names. I dug it, luxury's easy to get used to. What's hard is going in the other direction. I thought about the millions of people who'd be seeing me on TV this night. It was the biggest night of my life and I wanted to look good.

I took a shower and toweled-off, combed my hair and looked at myself in the hotel's wraparound mirrors. The make-up lights put out a bright light. My face was changing. I'd noticed it for months. I was looking better and better, getting more handsome by the day. Lemme say it straight-out, I was as vain as anybody, but this was more than vanity. My face was actually changing. Down to the cells. My eyes and nose, my mouth — all my features — were getting more distinct like a picture rising out of a fog. I'd asked Jessie about it. "You can look how you want, Elvis, that's part of it," is what he'd said.

e   *e*   *e*

I took a nap and got dressed for the show. I wore a tweed coat with metallic thread I'd picked up in New Orleans, with a black shirt and white tie, knotted in a loose Windsor, with charcoal-gray tuxedo pants and loafers. The coat was loud, you could've directed traffic with it, but I liked it. I couldn't see changing my hair or sideburns. My look had gotten me this far and nobody was trying to change me.

We took a cab over to CBS Studio 50 through a rainstorm. I rode with the Colonel. What a piece of work he was. The man was a two-ton destroyer wiping out anything in his path. I idolized the Colonel at this point and thought he was responsible for my success. Colonel Parker was the most competitive individual I ever met — more like a prize-fight manager than anything — and I was just glad he was on my side. The Colonel was from the old school — shirt hanging-out, pot gut, a five-dollar Cuban cigar in his mouth — this was before the business-school types had taken over the entertainment industry.

He blew smoke rings in the cab and looked straight ahead, told me with any kind of ratings the Dorseys would extend our contract — he didn't even ask what I was going sing this night — he told me "Heartbreak Hotel" was going gangbusters in Houston and New Orleans, the distributors were already reordering. I didn't think much about business; with the Colonel around I didn't have to.

The storm slammed our taxi sideways, but I didn't care, people were gonna be at home watching on TV.

Bill Randle, the big DJ out of Cleveland, was gonna introduce us. I liked Bill. He's the one who had gotten us the tryout with Arthur Godfrey the year before. "Everybody's gonna follow you, Elvis." That's what he'd said in Cleveland when we made a rock 'n' roll movie pilot for him, and now he was in New York introducing me.

The June Taylor Dancers opened the show playing xylophones, and then the camera panned to Bill Randle. Bill was a handsome guy, studious with a long, thin face and horn-rimmed glasses. "We'd like at this time," he said, "to introduce you to a young fellow who, like many performers — Johnnie Ray among them — came out of nowhere to be an overnight big star. This young fellow we saw for the first time while making a movie short." I was set to sprint on stage but wasn't sure how long Bill's introduction would take. "We think tonight he's going to make television history for you. We'd like for you to meet him now — Elvis Presley."

I wanted to give people a good show, something fast with a beat that'd wallop the camera. I stepped up to the mike and began "Shake, Rattle, and Roll," the Big Joe Turner song. People wanted something different, that was the only reason I was even on the show. I didn't back off an inch. I sang awhile and then pulled back with Scotty and Bill and danced to their riffs. I was boogeying pretty good and enjoying myself, I wasn't nervous at all once I got going. This all was a first for national TV, at least for a white guy; the kids understood, I knew that, the older generation I didn't know. The act was powerful, it was magic, although I didn't know then the how or why of it. A new Soul-form was gathering and I was part of it. I thought about joking a lyric, and then decided, no. People were seeing me where I'd never been, and in places I'd never see. I was so young and full of bullets.

More than anything, it was fun. The world was ready and Fate made me the lucky man. But it wasn't me. It was all of us, the Soul that flows upon the earth.

In the studio the red dot on the front of the camera glowed. I thought about people sitting in front of their TVs. Who was I to have everybody watching? The eye of the camera seemed to open and I went on to "Flip, Flop, and Fly." And now I was downhill racing, man. *"I'm a Mississippi bullfrog sitting on a hollow stump, got so many women I don't know where to jump."* What a silly lyric. Never could do it without cracking up. I got up on my toes and set my legs apart and cut loose. The girls in the studio were digging it. That was me, Elvis.

After the show we celebrated at the Roseland Ballroom with the Dorsey Brothers. I ate shrimp cocktails and talked about the show — I couldn't remember what happened — people had to tell me what I'd done. I couldn't sleep when I got back to the room. I felt like the bed was the tip of Mount Everest with the world spinning below. Downstairs, the morning delivery trucks were making noise, and dawn was creeping into the room.

Elvis Presley Online

elvispresleyonline.com

The award-winning Elvis Web site, developed by the author of *Clothed in Light*.

Listen to your favorite Elvis song in the *Elvis Discography*

Learn about Elvis in *Amazing Grace: The Elvis Multimedia Biography*

Add your story to the *Elvis Oral History Project*

Play the *Elvis Trivia Game*

Find an *Elvis Fan Club* in your area

Subscribe to the free *Elvis Presley Online Newsletter,* offering information about Elvis around the world